FAMILY

PRESSURE COOKER TIPS AND TIMINGS

FAMILY MATTERS

✓

PRESSURE COOKER TIPS AND TIMINGS

HILARY WALDEN

WARD LOCK

First published in 1990 by Ward Lock
Villiers House, 41/47 Strand, London WC2N 5JE

A Cassell imprint

© Ward Lock Limited 1990

Typeset by Columns of Reading

Printed and bound by Collins

British Library Cataloguing in Publication Data
Walden, Hilary
    Pressure cooker tips and timings.
    1. Food: Dishes prepared using pressure cookers. Recipes
    I. Title   II. Series
    641.587

    ISBN 0–7063–6908–4

INTRODUCTION

Although there are a number of different models of pressure cooker on the market, some fitted with refinements that simplify the operation, such as automatic pressure release, they all work on the same basic principle.

At normal atmospheric pressure, water boils at 100°C/212°F, and no matter how hard or for how long the water is boiled, the temperature will not rise. When the lid is properly fitted to a pressure cooker there is a complete seal between the lid and base. When water inside the cooker is brought to the boil, the steam can only escape through special devices and valves which control it. Pressure, therefore, builds up inside the cooker, increasing the temperature of the water and speeding up cooking. Also, steam is forced through food, cooking it.

Setting	Temperature
Steaming	100°C/212°F
5lb/Low pressure	109°C/228°F
10lb/Medium pressure	115°C/240°F
15lb/High pressure	121°C/250°F

Put the food in the cooker, with the trivet in place, if appropriate, and add the required amount of liquid (see individual entries) which must be one that produces steam, usually 300 ml/½ pint being the minimum. There must be sufficient space above the food after the cooker is loaded to allow the air to circulate, or foods to rise in the cooker during cooking.

Close the lid, making sure that it is fully locked in position – usually this is when the lid and body handles are aligned – put in place the correct weights or turn the cook- or steam-control knob to the appropriate setting, and place the cooker over a high heat until there is a good, steady stream of steam, and the correct number of visual indicators visible, if relevant for your type of cooker. The air inside the cooker will have been expelled and the air vent closed, allowing the steam produced by the hot liquid to accumulate and pressure inside the cooker to build up.

Adjust the heat beneath the cooker so that the steam escapes in a slow, steady stream, giving off a gentle hissing sound. If the steam escapes too quickly the cooker may boil dry before the completion of the cooking, whilst if there is insufficient steam, the temperature inside the cooker will not be high enough and the cooking of the food affected. If you notice that the flow of steam has ceased at any time during the cooking, immediately increase the heat beneath the cooker until the correct flow is returned and extend the cooking time slightly to compensate for the drop in temperature. During cooking, make sure that the cooker handles are not left over direct heat.

At the end of the cooking time, the pressure must be reduced, or released. This can be done in one of two ways, one quick, the other slow, depending on the food being cooked (see individual entries). Some of the most modern models are fitted with a variable pressure release system that allows the pressure to be released quickly without the need to use cold water.

These are general instructions for using a pressure cooker, but the instruction book provided with a cooker should be read carefully before it is used. If you do not have one for your cooker, contact the manufacturer.

If you would like to use the pressure cooker for cooking steamed puddings and preserves, choose a model that has three pressure controls – 5, 10 and 15 lb or Low, Medium and High – and if you plan to do any bottling, a domed lid will be necessary.

If you decide to buy a cooker with a single, or fixed weight, opt for a 15 lb model.

NOTE: All recipes serve four, unless otherwise stated.

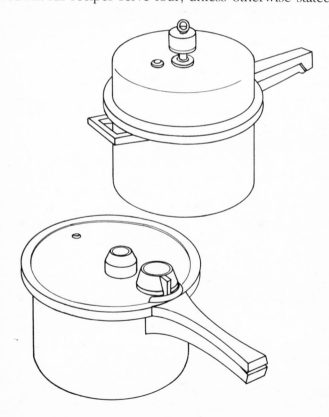

A–Z OF
PRESSURE COOKING

A

ADAPTING RECIPES

A pressure cooker can be used to cook many different types of dishes. The general points to bear in mind are that cooking times are reduced to about a third to a quarter of the original. Cooking times are governed by the size of the items to be cooked, not the amount. There must always be at least 300 ml/½ pint water in the cooker, and the longer the cooking, the more water is needed (see relevant entries).

If a particular food or dish is not included in this book, refer to one that is very similar, or choose an appropriate cooking method, such as casseroling.

ADZUKI BEANS

For general information about cooking Pulses, see page 114.

Pour sufficient boiling water over the beans to well cover and leave to soak for 1 hour. Drain, reserving liquid if it is to be used for cooking the beans, and make up to the required volume with water or stock.

Remove the trivet from the cooker, pour in 600 ml/ 1 pint water, stock or the reserved soaking liquid for every 225 g/8 oz adzuki beans. Do not add salt until after cooking otherwise it will toughen the beans and hamper the absorption of water. Bring to the boil, add beans, stir well and return to the boil. Skim the scum from the surface, adjust the heat so liquid is boiling, but the contents of cooker are not rising, fit the lid and, using the same heat, bring to 15 lb/High pressure. Adjust heat so that pressure is just maintained, and cook for 5 minutes. Reduce the pressure slowly, and drain beans. Flavour and season to taste.

ALMONDS, GROUND
Ground almonds can be used to quickly and lightly thicken the cooking liquid, give a different texture to the more commonly used flour-thickened sauces and at the same time give an interesting flavour to the dish. Commercially prepared ground almonds are convenient and simple to use, but if you have the time to freshly peel and grind whole almonds, they will make a sauce with a markedly better flavour and texture.

If the consistency of the cooking liquid is too thin, boil it until reduced. Purée the ground almonds with the cooking liquid, pour into the cooker and simmer, stirring occasionally until lightly thickened. Season to taste.

Make the sauce more luxurious by adding some single, whipping or double cream to it whilst boiling. Alternatively, once the sauce has lightly thickened, reduce the heat and stir in some plain yogurt (preferably strained Greek style) or fromage blanc and heat through, but do not allow to boil.

Ground almond sauces, particularly those finished with cream, yogurt or fromage blanc, seem to have a natural affinity with spices, especially those associated with India and the Middle East, such as cardamom, cinnamon, coriander seeds, allspice, ginger and fresh coriander.

Lamb in Almond Sauce Soak about 2.5 ml/½ tsp saffron strands in a little warm water. Heat about 30 ml/ 2 tbsp oil in the pressure cooker, add 575 g/1¼ lb boneless lean lamb, cut into large pieces, and cook quickly over a high heat, stirring occasionally, until a light even brown. Using a slotted spoon, transfer to absorbent kitchen paper and keep warm. Add a chopped large onion and finely crushed garlic clove to the cooker and cook, stirring occasionally, until softened but not coloured. Stir in the saffron liquid, 2.5 ml/½ tsp ground ginger, 2.5 ml/½ tsp ground allspice and 5 ml/ 1 tsp cinnamon and heat for 2 minutes. Stir in 350 ml/ 12 fl oz veal stock, bring to the boil, add the lamb, fit the lid and bring to 15 lb/High pressure. Cook for 3 minutes. Reduce the pressure quickly.

Meanwhile, fry approximately 40 g/1½ oz flaked almonds in a little butter until crisp and a light golden brown. Remove the lamb from the cooker, using a slotted spoon, and keep warm. Boil the cooking juices hard until reduced, then lower heat, stir in about 50 g/ 2 oz ground almonds and heat, stirring, until lightly thickened. Stir in 50 ml/2 fl oz double or whipping cream. Add approximately 10–15 ml/2–3 tsp orange flower water and seasoning to taste. Return meat to the cooker, stirring to coat in sauce. Transfer to a warmed serving dish and scatter over the almonds and some fresh coriander.

APPLES

Apples can be cooked in a number of different ways in a pressure cooker. Adjust the length of cooking according to the type of apple being cooked and the softness desired: softer-fleshed varieties should not be given as long as firm, crisp types. Cook at 10 lb/Medium pressure. (If the cooker you are using has only a single, 15 lb/High control, apples will cook more unevenly; remember to reduce the cooking times.)

Apple Slices Serve hot, or cold, with custard, ice cream, cream or yogurt, or use in crumbles, pies, tarts, pancakes and sweet omelettes.

Peel, core and cut apples into 1 cm/½ in thick slices and put into a heatproof container. Sprinkle with a little sugar and any flavourings (see below), then cover the container with a double thickness of greaseproof paper and tie securely in place. Place the trivet in the cooker, and pour in 300 ml/½ pint water. Bring to the boil. Add the fruit, using a 'lifting strap' (see page 77), or the separator basket, to lower into the container. Fit the lid and bring to 10 lb/Medium pressure, or 15 lb/High pressure if the cooker has only one pressure control. Cook for the required length of time, depending on the type of apple. Reduce the pressure quickly.

Cooking times at 15 lb/ High pressure	10 lb/ Medium pressure
In separator basket	
about 1½ minutes	2 minutes
In a container	
3–4 minutes	4 minutes

Bring apple to life by adding orange juice and grated orange rind, or sprinkling with spices, ground or whole, such as cloves, grated fresh nutmeg, chopped preserved ginger in syrup, or ground ginger, crushed cardamom seeds, or ground cinnamon.

Whole Apples Cored apples, with a line scored around them, can be cooked in the pressure cooker in 2½–3 minutes, depending on the size and type of apple. Filled with a sweet, or savoury stuffing they take about 3–4 minutes. They can be placed directly on the trivet, or in the separator basket. If cooking on the trivet, put the apples into the cooker before filling. To save leaving the filling behind when removing cooked apples from the cooker, lay a piece of foil or greaseproof paper under each apple on the trivet, and stand the unfilled apple on it, then add the filling. When cooking is complete, the filled apple can be lifted out on the foil or paper.

Almond Stuffed Apples Mix together 75 g/30 oz ground almonds, 5 ml/1 tsp honey, 25 g/1 oz softened, unsalted butter and the crushed seeds from 3 cardamom pods. Core 4 cooking apples and place in separator basket. Pack the filling tightly into apple cavities. Place the trivet in the cooker, pour in 300 ml/½ pint water and bring to the boil. Lower basket into the cooker, fit the lid and bring quickly to 15 lb/High pressure. Cook for 3–4 minutes, then reduce the pressure slowly. These apples are particularly good served with Dried Apricot Sauce, see page 13, or with orange flower water added.

Apple Purée Larger quantities of apples for puréeing can be cooked directly in the base of the cooker. Cut all the peeled and cored apples to the same size and put into the cooker, without the trivet in place, making sure the cooker is no more than half full when water is added. Do not pack apple down too tightly, otherwise it will not cook evenly. Sprinkle a little sugar over apple and add 300 ml/½ pint water. Fit the lid, bring to the boil and cook for 2–3 minutes at 10 lb/Medium, or 1½–2 minutes at 15 lb/High pressure. Reduce the pressure quickly unless cooker is half full, in which case reduce pressure slowly. Strain the apples and reduce cooking liquid by boiling. Do not add sweetening until the purée is to be used so that you can add the type and amount most suitable. Cook smaller amounts of apple for purées in a container (see Apple Slices), giving them a little extra cooking time.

Apple purée can be used for desserts, such as pies, tarts or crumbles, fools, whips, soufflés and sorbets; in apple cake recipes; for serving with milk or egg puddings; with ice cream, as a pancake filling, or made into sauces.

Apple Soufflé Sweeten 250 ml/8 fl oz thick apple purée to taste. If the purée is not thick enough, either boil it, stirring with a wooden spoon to drive off excess moisture, or blend 5 ml/1 tsp cornflour with a little water, stir into purée and cook, stirring with a wooden spoon until thickened. Beat the juice of ½ orange into the purée with about 2.5 ml/½ tsp ground cinnamon, a pinch grated nutmeg and 4 egg yolks. Whisk 4 egg whites, then lightly fold into apple mixture. Divide between 4 buttered dishes and bake at 220°C/425°F/gas 7 for 7–10 minutes until risen and golden. Serve with almond macaroons.

APRICOTS, DRIED

There is no need for natural dried apricots to be soaked overnight if they are to be cooked in a pressure cooker. About 10 minutes before apricots are to be cooked, pour boiling water over them, allowing 600 ml/1 pint water for each 450 g/1 lb of fruit. Cook, with the soaking liquor, in the base of the cooker, without the trivet in place. There must always be a minimum of 300 ml/½ pint liquid. Bring to 15 lb/High pressure and cook for 3 minutes. Reduce the pressure slowly.

Apricots that have been treated so they do not need soaking can be put directly into the cooker, with the same amount of water as ordinary dried apricots, and cooked for 2 minutes.

Add sugar and flavouring to taste – orange, cardamom, almonds, ginger and cinnamon are good partners for dried apricots. They can also be added to the dried apricots before they are cooked.

Dried Apricot Sauce Put 75 g/3 oz dried apricots (preferably not the treated no-need-to-soak type, as they tend to be on the sweet side) into a dish with 5 ml/1 tsp honey, 250 ml/8 fl oz dry white wine and 250 ml/8 fl oz water, or use all water. Cook as above. Remove apricots from liquor using a draining spoon. Boil liquor until reduced to about 300 ml/½ pint. Purée the fruit and liquor, pass through a sieve, if liked, to make a really smooth sauce. Add 10 ml/2 tsp orange flower water to give the sauce a very special flavour. Adjust the level of honey and add a little lemon juice to 'lift' the flavour, if necessary. Cover and chill.

APRICOTS, FRESH
For general information about cooking Fresh Fruit, see page 61.

Select firm, yet ripe apricots, cut them into halves and remove stones. Either place apricots in the separator basket or in a heatproof container, preferably in a single layer. Sprinkle with a little sugar and any flavourings, such as crushed cardamom or coriander seeds, a vanilla pod or orange juice, then cover the container with a double thickness of greaseproof paper and tie securely. Put the trivet in the cooker, pour in 300 ml/½ pint water and bring to the boil. Add fruit, using a 'lifting strap' (see page 77), or the separator basket, to lower into the container. Fit the lid and bring to 10 lb/Medium pressure, or 15 lb/High pressure if the cooker has only one pressure control. Cook for the required length of time (see below), depending on the hardness of the fruit. Reduce the pressure quickly. Remove and sweeten or flavour to taste, or use as required.

Cooking times at 15 lb/ High pressure	10 lb/ Medium pressure
In separator basket	
about 1 minute	1½–2 minutes
In a container	
2–2½ minutes	3½–4½ minutes

ARTICHOKES, GLOBE
For general information about cooking of Vegetables, see page 150.

Snap off the artichoke stalk at the base of head, then trim tops of leaves, using strong scissors. Put the trivet into the cooker, pour in 300 ml/½ pint liquid and bring to the boil. Stand artichokes on the trivet, or use the separator basket, fit the lid and bring to 15 lb/High pressure. Cook for the time given (see below), then reduce the pressure quickly. When cool enough to handle, open out the leaves and remove the central hairy 'choke'. Serve warm with melted unsalted butter or Hollandaise sauce; cold with mayonnaise, or fill the centre with prawns in a tomato flavoured mayonnaise.

Cooking times at 15 lb/High pressure

Small (about 225 g/8 oz)	7 minutes
Medium (about 275 g/10 oz)	9–10 minutes

ARTICHOKES, JERUSALEM

See Jerusalem Artichokes, page 72.

ASPARAGUS

For general information about cooking Vegetables, see page 150.

Cut the tougher, thicker ends of the spears from the quicker cooking, more tender, tips and cook separately. Put in the separator basket and bring 300 ml/½ pint water to the boil in the cooker before lowering in the basket. Young asparagus tips cook very quickly, and may require no more than 1 minute in the pressure cooker, older tips 1½–2 minutes, whilst stalks may take 2½–3½ minutes, depending on their age and size. Reduce the pressure quickly. Serve tips traditionally with Hollandaise sauce or melted butter, plus a wedge of lemon or orange, or tossed with melted, unsalted butter and freshly grated Parmesan cheese, or add an original touch and serve tossed with sesame seeds. The stalks can be used for purées, sauces and soups.

To blanch before freezing, bring to 10 lb/Medium or

15 lb/High pressure, if the cooker has only a single control, and reduce the pressure immediately. To serve as a vegetable, put the frozen asparagus into the cooker when the water is boiling, bring quickly to 10 lb/ Medium or 15 lb/High pressure, and reduce the pressure immediately. As frozen asparagus is very often softer than fresh, use it to make delicious soups and sauces.

AUBERGINES

A pressure cooker cooks aubergines much more quickly than conventional methods, so making it possible to prepare aubergine dishes in a few minutes; stuffed aubergines, for example, are ready in 2 minutes, and the flesh ready to make delicious purées and dips in about 6 minutes.

Stuffed Aubergines Cut 2 aubergines into half lengthways. Using a teaspoon, scoop out the flesh, leaving only a thin layer next to the skin; take care not to pierce the skin. Chop the flesh. Sauté a chopped large

onion in a little oil until softened and very lightly coloured, stir in the aubergine flesh and 100 g/4 oz chopped button mushrooms. Cook for 2–3 minutes over a fairly high heat, stirring occasionally, then add the flesh only of 3 chopped, skinned tomatoes and 30–45 ml/2–3 tbsp chopped parsley, freshly ground black pepper and a pinch of salt.

Pour 300 ml/½ pint water into the cooker and put the trivet in place. Place the aubergine shells in the separator basket (if they will not all fit, cook them in two batches). Divide the filling between the shells. Bring the water to the boil, lower in the separator basket, fit the lid and bring to 15 lb/High pressure and cook for 2 minutes. Reduce the pressure quickly. If liked, sprinkle a mixture of grated cheese and breadcrumbs over tops of aubergines and place under a hot grill until golden.

Aubergine Purée Cut an aubergine in half lengthways, then, using a sharp knife, score deep lines over the surface.

Pour 300 ml/½ pint water in the cooker, put the trivet in place and bring the water to the boil. Place the aubergines, flesh side uppermost, on the trivet, fit the lid, bring to 15 lb/High pressure and cook for about 6 minutes. Reduce the pressure quickly. Scoop the flesh into a blender or food processor and purée until smooth. Season and add lemon juice to taste; flavour with ground cumin, or crushed, lightly toasted cumin seeds, crushed garlic and/or chopped, softened onion. About 30 ml/2 tbsp olive oil can be gradually worked into the aubergine flesh whilst being puréed; or some strained Greek yogurt or fromage blanc added. Warm through gently, stirring, to serve as a sauce to accompany meats – especially lamb, or chicken; or serve cold as a dip, garnished with black olives and fresh coriander, or paprika instead if the purée has not been flavoured.

B

BACON

For general information about cooking Meat, see page 83: also Casseroling, page 38, and Pot Roasting, page 110.

Joints All joints of bacon up to about 1.25–1.4 kg/2½–3 lb can be cooked in the pressure cooker, but it is especially suitable for the cheaper cuts, such as slipper, flank, collar and streaky.

Modern sweet, and mild, cured bacon joints do not need to be soaked in cold water before cooking; simply place joint in base of cooker, cover with cold water, bring to the boil, then drain away water. Joints that have been cured in more traditional ways, especially large and smoked ones, should be soaked in cold water, in a cool place for about 2 hours, then drained and the water discarded.

Pour 300 ml/½ pint cold water into the cooker for a joint weighing up to 900 g/2 lb, plus an additional 150 ml/¼ pint water for the next 450 g/1 lb. Fit the lid, bring to 15 lb/High pressure and cook for 12 minutes per 450 g/1 lb. Reduce the pressure quickly.

For additional flavour, add some vegetables, such as an onion, carrot, celery or leek, plus a bouquet garni, or spices (such as cinnamon stick, cloves, or grated fresh ginger, or ground ginger) and black peppercorns. Dry cider, apple juice or white wine can replace the water, if wished.

The joint can be eaten as it is or prepared for baking once it is cool enough to handle. Strip off the skin and score the surface of fat with a sharp knife; press brown sugar into fat, or rub in honey, and stud with whole cloves. Place in an oven preheated to 200°C/ 400°F/gas 6 for 15 minutes to brown. Alternatively, press browned breadcrumbs into the fat. Serve hot, or leave until cold. If the cooking liquid is not too salty, skim it to remove excess fat, then thicken (see page 131) to make a sauce to serve with the joint.

Bacon joints can also be diced and used for making warming, economical casseroles.

Bacon Steaks and Chops Cook bacon steaks and chops surrounded by a liquid, as in a casserole or braise. Trim off excess fat before cooking and, if liked, fry in a little oil to brown, before pressure cooking.

Bacon Steaks (or Chops) with Apples and Cider Trim excess fat from 4 bacon steaks or chops. Remove the trivet from the cooker, add cored and thickly sliced apples, 2 blades of mace, a cinnamon stick and freshly ground black pepper and 300 ml/½ pint water. Bring to the boil, add the steaks or chops, fit the lid and bring to 15 lb/High pressure. Cook for about 6 minutes, depending on the thickness of the steaks. Reduce the pressure quickly.

Transfer the steaks or chops to a warmed plate, cover and keep warm. Boil the cooking liquid until reduced, remove the mace and cinnamon, and purée the liquid with the apple. Reheat, stirring, and boil, if necessary, to thicken further. Finish the sauce by gradually stirring in a few small knobs of butter, a few spoonfuls of double cream or 50–75 g/2–3 oz fromage blanc (if fromage blanc is added, keep the sauce below boiling point). Adjust the seasoning and pour over the bacon. Garnish with fresh apple slices, chopped walnuts or parsley.

Boil-in-the-Bag Joints Cut the top corner of bag to prevent bag bursting. Place joint (in the bag) on the trivet, add the same amount of water, per 450 g/1 lb weight as for an ordinary joint, fit the lid, bring to 15 lb/High pressure and cook for the same length of time as for an ordinary joint.

BARLEY

For general information about cooking Grains, see page 64.

Remove the trivet from the cooker and pour in 600 ml/1 pint water or stock for every 100 g/4 oz of barley. Bring to the boil, stir in the barley and return to the boil. If using water, add some vegetables and herbs for flavour. Adjust the heat so the liquid is boiling but the contents not rising in the cooker. Fit the lid then, maintaining the same heat, bring to 15 lb/High pressure. Cook pot barley (the barley grain from which only the outer husk has been removed) for about 20 minutes, pearl barley (which has the bran as well as the husk removed) for 7–8 minutes. Reduce the pressure slowly. Drain the barley and season and flavour as required.

BASMATI RICE

Basmati is an Indian long-grain rice that is traditionally used for pilaus and the drier biryanis. Basic cooking techniques are as long-grain rice (see page 121).

Pilau Heat 30 ml/2 tbsp ghee or oil in the pressure cooker, stir in a finely chopped onion and cook, stirring occasionally, until browned. Stir in a crushed garlic clove and cook for 1–2 minutes. Crush 4 cloves, 8 cardamom pods and a 5 cm/2 inch piece of cinnamon together, then add to the cooker with 2 bay leaves and 225 g/8 oz basmati rice. Cook for 2–3 minutes. Stir in 900 ml/1½ pints chicken or vegetable stock, or water, bring to the boil, adjust the heat so the liquid is boiling but the contents of the cooker are not rising, fit the lid and bring to 15 lb/High pressure, over the same heat. Adjust the heat so the pressure is just maintained, and cook for 2 minutes.

Meanwhile, fry 50 g/2 oz shelled pistachio nuts or halved, blanched almonds in a little oil until golden.

Reduce the pressure slowly. Strain the rice, remove spices and bay leaves, return rice to rinsed cooker placed over a very low heat and fluff the rice up with a fork, adding the nuts, 50 g/2 oz sultanas, a few drops of orange flower water, if liked, and seasoning to taste.

BEANS, DRIED

See Pulses, page 114, and individual types such as borlotti and butter.

BEANS, BROAD, FRENCH and RUNNER

For general information about cooking Vegetables, see page 150.

The best way to cook fresh beans is in a separator basket as it will then be easier to put them into, and take them from, the cooker. French beans cook very quickly so should be topped and tailed and left whole. Really fresh, young runner beans do not take long either, so, to help keep them crisp, simply top and tail and remove any side strings, but do not cut them too small before cooking. Cut tougher, more stringy runner beans into normal lengths, after topping and tailing. Bring 300 ml/ ½ pint water in the cooker to the boil before adding the beans and cook for times given (see below). Reduce the pressure quickly.

Cooking times at 15 lb/High pressure

French beans	2–3 minutes
Young runner beans	3 minutes
Older runner beans	4 minutes

Broad Beans, see page 21.

BEEF

For general information about cooking Meat, see page 83. A pressure cooker is most suitable for cooking mid-price, therefore mid-quality cuts of beef, such as topside, silverside and chuck steak, rather than prime ones like fillet, or the cheaper cuts, such as tougher stewing steak, shin, flank, etc.

Marinating in wine, beer, cider, yogurt or citrus juice, herbs and seasonings for a few hours in a cool place will help both the tenderness and the flavour; the tougher the cut, the more important marinating becomes, and, if possible, it should last about 8 hours. Trim off gristle and surplus fat before cooking.

Pot Roasting Beef For general information, see page 110.

The size of the joint determines the length of cooking rather than the toughness of the joint; extending the time will only make the meat drier on the outside and more difficult to chew – marinating overnight is a more effective course of action. For the same reason, it is advisable to use joints less than about 1.25 kg/2½ lb.

Pot roast beef joints for 12–15 minutes per 450 g/1 lb at 15 lb/High pressure.

Caseroling Beef For general information, see page 38. Cut meat into large, bite-size pieces, or slices about 3 cm/1¼ inch thick. Trim well of fat and gristle.

Carbonnade of Beef Over a high heat, quickly brown both sides of 4 trimmed slices of chuck steak in butter and oil in the base of the cooker. Transfer to absorbent kitchen paper. Sauté 2 sliced onions and a garlic clove in the cooker until soft and a light golden brown. Stir in 1 diced red pepper and 100 g/4 oz thickly sliced button mushrooms, cook for 1–2 minutes, then stir in 5 ml/1 tsp brown sugar, 15 ml/1 tbsp wine vinegar, 15 ml/1 tbsp tomato purée, 15 ml/1 tbsp wholegrain mustard, a bouquet garni and 300 ml/½ pint brown ale. Bring to the boil, return the beef to the cooker, fit the lid and bring to 15 lb/High pressure. Cook for about 5 minutes. Reduce the pressure slowly.

Transfer beef to a warmed plate and keep warm. Blend 15 ml/1 tbsp plain flour with a little water, then stir into the cooker. Bring to the boil, stirring, and simmer for 2 minutes. Season and adjust the levels of mustard, tomato and sweetness, if necessary. Remove the bouquet garni and pour liquid over beef.

BEETROOT

Beetroot normally take a long time to cook, but in a

pressure cooker they will be done in 10–20 minutes, depending on size. For general information about cooking vegetables, see page 150.

Wash the beetroot carefully to avoid damaging the skin, place in the cooker, without the trivet, and add 600 ml/1 pint water if the beetroot are small, 900 ml/1½ pints if medium and 1.1 litre/2 pints if large. Fit the lid, bring to 15 lb/High pressure and cook for 10–20 minutes, depending on size. Reduce the pressure slowly.

Lift beetroot from cooker, then peel. Although beetroot are most often served cold, with salads, they make a delicious hot vegetable. Cut a small slice from the top, dot with a knob of butter or a spoonful of soured cream, sprinkle with a little seasoning, and chopped chives or caraway seeds, if liked. Alternatively, toss with melted butter simmered with a little orange juice and grated orange rind.

BLACKBERRIES For general information about cooking Fruit, see page 62.

Whether to use a pressure cooker for cooking blackberries depends on the firmness of the fruit, and personal preference. Cultivated blackberries are usually soft and juicy, and quickly collapse when cooked, so are really best cooked gently and briefly by conventional methods. The same applies to some wild berries, but firmer ones can be cooked in a pressure cooker in a very short time.

Clean the fruit gently and put into a heatproof container. Sprinkle a little sugar over and cover the container with foil or a double thickness of greaseproof paper. Tie securely in place. Place the trivet in the cooker and pour in 300 ml/½ pint water and bring to the boil. Using a 'lifting strap' (see page 77) or the separator basket, lower the dish of fruit into the cooker, fit the lid and bring to 10 lb/Medium or 15 lb/High pressure, if your cooker does not have a three-pressure control. Cook for about 1 or 2 minutes respectively, depending on the juiciness of the fruit. Reduce the pressure quickly.

Blackberry Sauce Cook 225 g/8 oz blackberries with a cinnamon stick, 2 cloves, 75 ml/3 fl oz water and 15 ml/ 1 tbsp suger sprinkled over, as above. Remove the spices, then purée the fruit and juice and pass through a non-metallic sieve.

Blend 7.5 ml/1½ tsp arrowroot with 30 ml/2 tbsp water. Stir in the blackberry purée, then pour into a small pan and bring to the boil, stirring. Add 30 ml/ 2 tbsp port and simmer for 1–2 minutes. Taste for sweetness and sharpness, adding sugar or lemon juice, as necessary. Serve with plain cakes or puddings, or with duck.

BLACKCURRANTS

For general information about cooking Fruit, see page 62.

Clean the fruit gently and put into a heatproof container. Sprinkle a little sugar over and cover the container with foil or a double thickness of greaseproof paper. Tie securely in place. Place the trivet in the cooker and pour in 300 ml/½ pint water. Using a 'lifting strap' (see page 77), or the separator basket, lower the dish of fruit into the cooker and fit the lid. Bring to 15 lb/High or 10 lb/Medium pressure, if your cooker has a three-pressure control. Cook for about 2 minutes, depending on the softness of the fruit. Reduce the pressure quickly.

Blackcurrant Flummery Cook 225 g/8 oz blackcurrants with about 25 g/1 oz sugar as above. Purée and sieve the fruit. Stir in 5 ml/1 tsp lemon juice and add sugar to taste. When cold, stir in 75 ml/3 fl oz plain yogurt. Whip 150 ml/5 fl oz double cream until soft peaks form, then fold in blackcurrant purée. Whisk 2 egg whites until stiff but not dry and fold into the blackcurrant mixture. Spoon into 4 cold glasses and chill lightly. Serve decorated with sprigs of mint or flaked almonds, and accompanied by crisp biscuits.

BLANCHING
Vegetables are blanched prior to freezing to extend their freezer storage life, because blanching slows down the activity of natural enzymes present in vegetables, that causes deterioration of the colour, texture, flavour and nutritional value.

Using a pressure cooker for blanching reduces both the time taken and the amount of water needed. Follow the steps for cooking vegetables (see page 150) but only bring the pressure to 10 lb/Medium pressure. Blanch for the recommended time and reduce the pressure quickly. Immediately cool the vegetables under cold running water. When cold, drain well.

BOIL-IN-THE-BAG
A pressure cooker can be used for cooking frozen foods, such as casseroles and fish in sauce, that are packed in boiling bags. Pierce the bag near one of the seams, stand the bag, with the pierced seam upwards, in a separator basket. Pour 300 ml/½ pint water into the pressure cooker, place the separator in the cooker, fit

the lid and bring quickly to 15 lb/High pressure. Cut the cooking time specified on the packet by half. Reduce the pressure quickly.

BORLOTTI BEANS

For general information about cooking Pulses, see page 114.

Pour sufficient boiling water over the beans to well cover them, and leave to soak for an hour. Drain, reserving the liquid if it is to be used for cooking the beans, and make up to the required volume with water or stock.

Remove the trivet from the cooker, add the beans and 900 ml/1½ pints water, stock or the reserved soaking liquid for every 225 g/8 oz beans. Do not add salt until after cooking otherwise it will toughen the beans and hamper the absorption of water. Bring to the boil, remove the scum from the surface, adjust the heat so the liquid is boiling but the contents of the cooker are not rising, fit the lid and bring to 15 lb/High pressure, over the same heat. Adjust heat so the pressure is just maintained, and cook for 15 minutes. Reduce the pressure slowly. Drain the beans; flavour and season to taste.

Borlotti beans have an affinity with olive oil and lemon juice and a salad that is quick, simple, and delicious can be made by tossing the warm beans with a dressing of twice as much olive oil as lemon juice, and freshly chopped parsley, plus some chopped onion and garlic, if liked. Leave to cool, then chill lightly. Or make into a more substantial, colourful salad, as follows.

Borlotti Bean, Red Pepper and Cheese Salad Pour boiling water over 100 g/4 oz borlotti beans and leave to soak for 1 hour. Drain the beans. Put into the pressure cooker with 900 ml/1½ pints water. Bring to the boil, remove the scum from the surface and adjust the heat so the contents boil but do not rise. Fit the lid and bring to

15 lb/High pressure, over the same heat. Adjust heat so the pressure is just maintained and cook for 10 minutes. Reduce the pressure slowly. Drain the beans.

Whisk together 60 ml/4 tbsp olive oil, 30 ml/2 tbsp lemon juice, 15 ml/1 tbsp chopped parsley, 7.5 ml/ 1½ tsp wholegrain mustard, a finely crushed garlic clove and seasonings, then stir into the beans while they are still warm. Leave to cool, then toss with a diced red pepper and 100 g/4 oz crumbled feta or goats' cheese.

Place some crisp lettuce leaves in a shallow bowl and add the bean salad. Scatter with crisp croûtons and toss lightly.

BOTTLING

Bottling is a traditional method used in the home for preserving fruits. Vegetables should not be bottled domestically as they do not have the necessary acid content, and cannot be brought to a sufficiently high temperature to make them safe for long-term storage. Tomatoes, usually thought of as a vegetable, are, in fact, a fruit and can be bottled. As when frozen, tomatoes collapse when bottled, but if you have glut of them preserve them by bottling rather than freezing to save on precious freezer space.

Bottling fruit in a pressure cooker is by far the quickest method, and it is also the easiest to control exactly, therefore the safest. The cooker must have a 5 lb/Low pressure control. Bottling jars up to 450 g/1 lb in size will fit into any type of pressure cooker, but a cooker with a domed lid will be needed for larger bottling jars.

The fruit should be ripe, but firm and in good condition. For evenness of cooking, use fruit that is a similar size and ripeness.

Check that the bottles are not damaged in any way and that the rings are sound, flexible and fit snugly on the bottles. Also make sure that the bottles will fit easily into the cooker when standing on the trivet, and are not touching the lid, sides or each other.

Pack the fruit well into the warm, clean bottles, without squashing it, to prevent it rising after processing. The fruit may be preserved in water or in a sugar syrup, which will give a better flavour and colour. To make the syrup, dissolve 225 g/8 oz sugar in 600 ml/1 pint water; place over gentle heat and bring to the boil for 1 minute.

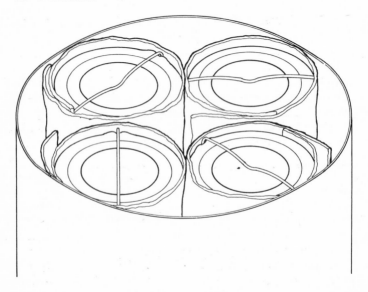

Slowly pour boiling syrup or water into the bottles, adding a little at a time and frequently tapping the bottle on the work surface to free any air bubbles. Fill to within 2 cm/¾ inch of top of bottles. Fit the rubber bands onto the necks, then the glass caps or metal discs, clips or screw bands, screwing these tight, then turning back by quarter of a turn.

Put the trivet into the cooker, add 900 ml/1½ pints water, plus 5 ml/1 tsp vinegar. Bring to the boil, then pack bottles into the cooker, packing newspaper between them to make sure they do not touch. Fit the lid on the cooker and bring to 5 lb/Low pressure over a moderate heat. Adjust the heat so this pressure is maintained and cook for the time given below. Turn off the heat, or remove cooker carefully from heat and allow the pressure to reduce slowly.

Cooking times at 5lb/Low pressure

Apples, peeled, quartered or thickly sliced	1 minute
Apricots, pricked	1 minute
Cherries	1 minute
Damsons, pricked	1 minute
Pears (eating), peeled and halved	3 minutes
Pears (cooking), peeled and halved	5 minutes
Plums, pricked	1 minute
Rhubarb, cut into 5 cm/2 inch lengths	1 minute
Soft fruits (leave overnight covered with sugar syrup, see above. Drain, reserving syrup, pack fruit into jars and cover with the reserved syrup)	about 1 minute

One by one, lift the jars from the cooker, place on a wooden surface and tighten the screw bands. When cool, remove the screw bands or clips and lift the bottle by the cap or disc to make sure a vacuum has been formed, and the bottle hermetically sealed. If the lid or cap holds firm, replace the screw band or clip, having first rubbed in some oil to prevent rust forming, label and store in a cool, dark, dry place.

Bottled Tomatoes Whole, unskinned tomatoes must be small or medium and even-sized, ripe yet firm. Wipe, remove the stalks, then pack tomatoes into jars. Fill up with a brine solution made with 15 g/½ oz salt per 1.1 litres/2 pints water, and add 10 ml/2 tsp lemon juice, or 2.5 ml/¼ tsp citric acid to each 450 g/1 lb jar. Pressure cook at 5 lb/Low pressure for 5 minutes.

For solid pack tomatoes no liquid is added and tomatoes of any size can be used, but they must be firm. Skin the tomatoes. Small fruit can be left whole but larger ones should be halved or quartered so they can be packed tightly, leaving no air spaces. To each 450 g/ 1 lb jar, add 5 ml/1 tsp salt, 2.5 ml/½ tsp sugar and either 10 ml/2 tsp lemon juice or 1.25 ml/¼ tsp citric acid, sprinkling them over the tomatoes as they are packed into the jar. Pressure cook at 5 lb/Low pressure for 15 minutes. Reduce pressure slowly.

For tomatoes bottled in their own juice, skin and pack firm tomatoes into jars. Simmer extra tomatoes with 5 ml/1 tsp salt to every 900 g/2 lb tomatoes, in a covered pan. Strain the juice into the jars, adding 10 ml/2 tsp lemon juice or 1.25 ml/½ tsp citric acid to every 450 g/ 1 lb jar. Pressure cook at 5 lb/Low pressure for 5 minutes. Reduce the pressure slowly.

BREAD

Bread is not cooked in a pressure cooker, but many dishes containing bread are most successful and are cooked in a fraction of the time taken when cooked conventionally. Breadcrumbs can be used to thicken cooking liquids.

Fluffy Cheese Pudding Pour 300 ml/¼ pint milk over 50 g/2 oz wholemeal or granary breadcrumbs and leave to soak for 1 hour. Beat in 100 g/4 oz soft cheese with herbs, 75 g/3 oz grated full-flavoured cheese, 2 egg yolks, 10 ml/2 tsp Dijon mustard and freshly ground black pepper. Whisk 2 egg whites until stiff but not dry, then lightly fold into cheese mixture until just evenly combined. Turn into a buttered, heatproof dish and cover dish with a dome of oiled side down foil. Pour 600 ml/1 pint water into the pressure cooker and put the trivet into the cooker. Stand dish on the trivet, fit the lid and bring to 15 lb/High pressure and cook for 20 minutes.

Meanwhile, fry 45–60 ml/3–4 tbsp breadcrumbs until crisp and browned.

Reduce the pressure slowly. Remove the dome of foil and scatter with breadcrumbs. Serve immediately.

Savoury Bread Pudding Spread 4 slices of granary, wholemeal or rye bread thinly with peanut butter, tahini or butter. Remove the crusts.

Layer bread with 3 sliced tomatoes and 75 g/3 oz mature Cheddar cheese in a buttered ovenproof dish. Beat 300 ml/½ pint milk into 100 g/4 oz soft cheese, flavoured with herbs and garlic, if liked, strain in 2 lightly beaten eggs, add black pepper, to taste, then pour over the bread. Leave to soak for 20–30 minutes.

Cover the dish with foil or a double thickness of greaseproof paper and secure tightly. Pour 300 ml/½ pint water into the pressure cooker and put the trivet in place. Using a lifting strap (see page 77) or the separator basket, lower the dish onto the trivet, fit the lid and bring to 15 lb/High pressure and cook for 10 minutes. Reduce the pressure slowly.

Mix 25 g/1 oz grated cheese and 30 ml/2 tbsp porridge oats together and sprinkle over the top of the pudding. Place under a hot grill until golden. Leave to stand for 2 minutes before serving.

BROAD BEANS

For general information about cooking Vegetables, see page 150.

The best way to cook broad beans is in a separator

basket to that it will be easy to put them into, and take them from, the cooker. With the trivet in place, pour 300 ml/½ pint water into the cooker, bring to the boil, lower in the beans and fit the lid. Bring to 15 lb/High pressure and cook for 3–4 minutes, depending on size, age and tenderness. Reduce the pressure quickly.

Blanch broad beans prior to freezing at 10 lb/Medium pressure for 1 minute, or 45 seconds at 15 lb/High pressure. Cook in pressure cooker from frozen for 2–3 minutes at 15 lb/High pressure.

Summer savory and tarragon compliment broad beans. The beans also go well with bacon, fried until just crisp, or ham with some cream poured over the bacon and beans then simmered for a few minutes. Or, more simply, add some strained Greek yogurt and warm through gently. Delicious, too, with prawns to make a cold salad, especially if a lemony dressing, such as a light mayonnaise (made with a whole egg instead of an egg yolk) is added.

BROCCOLI

For general information about cooking Vegetables, see page 150.

Because the florets cook more quickly than the stalks, the two parts must be cooked separately to avoid overcooked florets or under-cooked stems. Cook florets for 1½–2½ minutes, small spears for about 2½ minutes and stalks, which can be used for soups, for 3–3½ minutes.

Blanch for freezing (see page 25) at 10 lb/medium pressure for 1 minute or for 45 seconds at 15 lb/High pressure. Cook from frozen at 15 lb/High pressure for about 45 seconds. Reduce pressure quickly. Serve broccoli tossed with melted butter or olive oil and lemon juice, or scattered with crumbled blue cheese or toasted flaked almonds.

BRUSSELS SPROUTS

For general information about cooking Vegetables, see page 150.

Choose sprouts that are all the same size, and cook small ones for 1½–2 minutes; medium sized ones for 2–3 minutes; large ones 3–3½ minutes. Blanch for freezing (see page 25) at 10 lb/Medium pressure for 1 minute. Cook from frozen at 15 lb/high pressure for 1–1½ minutes.

Toss cooked Brussels sprouts with cooked chestnuts, butter-fried flaked almonds or toasted sesame seeds and plain yogurt.

Brussels Sprouts with Cashew Nut Sauce Fry a chopped onion, a garlic clove and 10 ml/2 tsp grated fresh root ginger until soft, then stir in the crushed seeds of 2 cardamom pods and 50 g/2 oz cashew nuts and cook until the nuts are a light golden brown.

Meanwhile, put the trivet into the pressure cooker and pour in 300 ml/½ pint vegetable stock and bring to the boil. Put 450 g/1 lb even-sized small sprouts in the separator basket and lower into the cooker. Fit the lid and bring to 15 lb/High pressure. Cook for 1–2 minutes. Reduce the pressure quickly. Transfer sprouts to a warmed serving dish, cover and keep warm. Remove trivet from cooker, add 75 ml/3 fl oz medium bodied, dry white wine or stock, if liked, then boil hard until reduced to 100 ml/4 fl oz. Put the nut mixture into a blender and purée, gradually adding the reduced liquor. Pour back into the cooker and reheat gently, stirring in 150 ml/¼ pint double cream, or fromage blanc, and about 10 ml/2 tsp garam masala, or to taste. Season, then pour over the sprouts and scatter with 15 ml/1 tbsp cashew nuts, lightly fried in butter.

BUTTER BEANS

For general information about cooking Pulses, see page 114.

Pour sufficient boiling water over the butter beans to well cover and leave to soak for 1 hour. Drain, reserving the liquid if it is to be used for cooking the butter beans, and make up to the required volume with water or stock.

Remove the trivet from the cooker, add the beans and 900 ml/1½ pints water, stock or the reserved soaking liquid for every 225 g/8 oz butter beans. Do not add salt until after cooking otherwise it will toughen the beans and hamper the absorption of water. Bring to the boil, skim the scum from the surface, adjust the heat so the liquid is boiling but the contents of the cooker are not rising, fit the lid and, maintaining the same heat, bring to 15 lb/High pressure. Adjust heat so the pressure is just maintained, and cook for 15 minutes. Reduce the pressure slowly, and drain the butter beans. Flavour and season to taste.

Butter Bean Dip Cover 225 g/8 oz butter beans with plenty of boiling water and leave to soak for 1 hour. Drain. Cook as above. Reduce the pressure slowly.

Purée beans with 10 ml/2 tsp ground cumin, the juice of 2 large lemons, 2 crushed garlic cloves and 30 ml/2 tbsp chopped fresh coriander. Season to taste. Transfer to a bowl, cover and chill. Garnish with fresh coriander and olives, or scatter over crumbled sharp blue cheese, feta or goats' cheese, and serve with hot pitta bread or warm Granary or wholemeal bread.

C

CAKES

As cakes are often made from the same type of mixtures that are used for puddings, perfectly acceptable cakes can be cooked in the pressure cooker. However, unless you do not have any other means of cooking, or really do not want to turn the oven on for a single cake, there is no advantage in using the pressure cooker as it will not save any time. Also, the cakes will lack the characteristic colour of a baked cake, although this can be camouflaged by adding coffee or chocolate to the cake mixture, or covering the cooked cake with icing.

Any type of heatproof container that will fit inside the cooker can be used; cakes will cook more quickly in cake or loaf tins, and in rectangular tins rather than square or round cake tins.

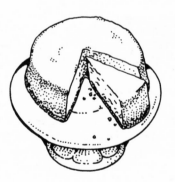

Base the cooking time on that of a 'steamed' pudding made from a similar weight of mixture – for example, cook a cake made from a 2-egg quantity of a creamed mixture for the same length of time as you would a pudding made from a 2-egg quantity of creamed mixture, and follow the same steps of covering, pre-steaming, cooking at 5 lb/Low pressure and reducing the pressure slowly. Remove the loaf or cake tin from the cooker, leave it to stand for 5 minutes, then turn out onto a wire rack to cool.

Coffee and Walnut Cake Beat together 100 g/4 oz unsalted butter or margarine with 100 g/4 oz demerara sugar until light and fluffy. Gradually beat in 2 beaten eggs and about 15 ml/1 tbsp coffee granules, then fold in 150 g/5 oz self-raising flour and 50 g/2 oz chopped walnuts. Spoon into a non-stick, or buttered 450 g/1 lb loaf tin, or 15 cm/6 inch deep, round tin.

Smooth the surface, place a double thickness of greaseproof paper (pleated across the centre) loosely over the tin and tie securely in place. Put the trivet into the cooker, pour in 600 ml/1 pint water, bring to the boil then, using a 'lifting strap' (see page 77), lower in the loaf or cake tin. Fit the lid without the weights in place, or with the pressure control switched to 'open' and pre-steam for 15 minutes. Bring to 5 lb/Low pressure and cook for 30 minutes. Reduce the pressure slowly.

Remove the tin from cooker, leave to stand for 5 minutes, then turn out onto a wire rack to cool. If liked, cover with coffee icing and decorate with walnut halves.

To make the icing, mix together 10–15 ml/2–3 tsp instant coffee granules and 100 g/4 oz sieved icing sugar, then blend in approximately 10–20 ml/2–4 tsp warm water to make a smooth icing that will coat the back of a spoon. Spread immediately over cake.

Honey, Lemon and Spice Cake Slowly bring 600 ml/1 pint water to the boil in pressure cooker. Meanwhile, melt together 175 ml/6 fl oz honey and 50 g/2 oz diced unsalted butter. Sieve into a bowl, 225 g/8 oz self-raising flour, 5 ml/1 tsp mixed spice, and

5 ml/1 tsp bicarbonate of soda. Form a well in the centre, pour in the honey mixture and start to beat all the ingredients together. When partially mixed, include 2 lightly beaten eggs and the rind and juice of 1 lemon. When smooth, pour into a well-buttered 15 cm/6 inch deep, round cake tin. Cover the top of the tin with a double thickness of greaseproof paper and tie securely in place. Put the trivet into the cooker and using a 'lifting strap' (see page 77), lower the tin into the cooker. Fit the lid without the weights in place, or with the steam outlet control set at 'open'. Pre-steam for 25 minutes. Fit the weights, or close the steam control outlet, increase the heat beneath the cooker and bring the pressure to 5 lb/Low pressure. Cook for about 23 minutes. Reduce the pressurer slowly.

Remove cake tin from the cooker and allow to cool for about 10 minutes before inverting onto a wire cooling rack to cool.

CARROTS

For general information about cooking Vegetables, see page 150.

Trim, scrape or peel, and cut as required. Cook in the separator basket, or on the trivet, but do not add to the cooker until the 300 ml/½ pint water is boiling. Reduce the pressure quickly.

Cooking times at 15 lb/High pressure

Whole, slim young carrots	about 2–3 minutes
Halved or quartered old carrots	about 4 minutes
Large chunks	about 2 minutes
Slices, 1 cm/½ inch thick	about 2 minutes

Blanch before freezing at 10 lb/Medium pressure, if available, for 1 minute; if only 15 lb/High pressure is available, blanch for about 45 seconds. Cook from frozen in pressure cooker for 1–1½ minutes, depending on age and size.

CASSEROLES

For general information about cooking Meat, see page 83. Also, individual types of meat – beef, pork, lamb.

Middle quality cuts of meat are most suitable for casseroling in the pressure cooker. Cooking for an extended time in the pressure cooker will not make really tough meat truly tender – the pieces of meat may fall apart, but they will still be tough to eat. For the best results it is necessary to achieve a balance between softening the pieces of meat, and preventing them from becoming chewy, dry and tasteless. The meat will benefit from marinating in wine, cider, beer or plain yogurt to help tenderize it; the flavour will also be improved if herbs and spices are included. The taste will also be improved if the casserole is cooked (or, preferably, slightly undercooked) in advance, and kept in a cool place overnight to allow flavours to mature and meld together.

Cut the meat into large, bite-sized cubes, or slices about 3 cm/1¼ inch thick. For even cooking, use pieces that are all the same size. Frying meat in hot fat first to brown it, starts to cook it. Whereas this will have little effect on the cooking of large pieces of meat, it can make a difference to small pieces, especially if the browning is more than a quick sear in hot fat, not only because the cooking process has begun, but also because the meat will already be heated through when pressure cooking starts. If the meat has been marinated, drain off the marinade well and be sure to dry the meat on absorbent kitchen paper before browning. Although browning of the meat is often believed to seal the juices inside it, this has been shown not to be the case; it does, however, produce a more savoury flavour and richer colour.

The ingredients cannot be stirred during cooking so use a thin cooking liquid, such as stock, as a thick liquid may 'catch' on the bottom of the cooker. Canned sauces and soups should be thinned down with a little water, stock, or wine, before being added.

If meat is coated with seasoned flour before being browned prior to pressure cooking, check the consistency of the liquid before fitting the lid to make sure it is sufficiently thin. As there is no evaporation during cooking, less liquid should be added than when cooking by conventional means, although there must always be a minimum of 300 ml/½ pint of a liquid to produce steam, such as water, stock, wine or beer.

Generally, the meat or vegetables are no more than half covered by the liquid. Bring the liquid to the boil in the cooker before adding the meat to it, and bring as quickly as possible to 15 lb/High pressure to minimize the shrinkage of meat. The cooker must never be more than half full when all the ingredients have been added. After cooking, reduce the pressure quickly, unless a particular recipe specifies to the contrary. There are many ways that the liquid can be thickened after cooking, see page 139.

Using a pressure cooker is an economical way of cooking large amounts of casseroles as it is the size of the pieces of meat, not the quantity, that determines the cooking time.

Beef Casserole Cut 575 g/1¼ lb top rump or blade steak into even, large bite-size pieces. If liked, marinate the beef in a cool place for 4–8 hours in 200–300 ml/ 7 fl oz–¼ pint red wine, 4 crushed black peppercorns, a bay leaf, a large sprig parsley, and a chopped onion. Drain the marinade from the meat, and pat the meat dry with absorbent kitchen paper.

Remove the trivet from the cooker, heat a little oil in cooker, add the beef and cook briefly over a high heat, stirring occasionally until lightly browned. Using a slotted spoon, transfer meat to absorbent kitchen paper. Reduce heat to low, add a chopped onion and 3 chopped bacon rashers and cook, stirring occasionally, until softened. Stir in 2 carrots and 2 sticks celery, cut into large chunks, 100 g/4 oz button mushrooms and 8 shallots. Add 174 ml/6 fl oz each red wine and brown veal stock, a bay leaf, 3 sprigs parsley and 2 of thyme. Bring to the boil; return meat to cooker.

Fit the lid, bring to 15 lb/High pressure and cook for 5 minutes. Reduce the pressure quickly.

Using a slotted spoon transfer meat and vegetables to a warm serving dish and keep warm. Discard herbs; whisk into liquid in cooker 15 ml/1 tbsp butter blended with 15 ml/1 tbsp plain flour, bring to the boil while stirring, then simmer until thickened. Taste and adjust seasoning. Return meat and vegetables to cooker, stir to coat with the sauce and serve sprinkled with chopped parsley.

CAULIFLOWER

For general information about cooking Vegetables, see page 150.

Cauliflowers are best cooked divided into florets, because if left whole the florets would be overcooked before the centre was tender. (Trimmings need not be wasted as they can be cooked separately to make into purées, or used for soup.)

Place the florets in the separator basket. Put the trivet into the cooker and pour in 300 ml/½ pint water, bring to the boil. Add the separator basket, fit the lid, bring to 15 lb/High pressure and cook for approximately 1–2 minutes. Reduce the pressure quickly.

Blanch for freezing for 1 minute at 10 lb/Medium pressure, if available, otherwise for about 45 seconds at 15 lb/High pressure. To cook from frozen, make sure all the florets are separate, and cook for about 1 minute at 15 lb/High pressure.

CELERIAC

For general information about cooking Vegetables, see page 150.

Celeriac belongs to the same family as celery and does have a faintly similar flavour, but its texture is nearer that of a potato. Using a vegetable knife, thickly peel away the skin. Cut the vegetable into even-sized 2–2.5 cm/¾–1 inch cubes or 1 cm/½ inch thick slices. Cook immediately, or put into cold water with lemon juice added to prevent discoloration. Place celeriac in the separator basket. Put trivet into the cooker and pour in 300 ml/½ pint water, bring to the boil, add the separator basket, fit the lid, bring to 15 lb/High pressure and cook for the given time (see below). Reduce the pressure quickly. Toss with unsalted butter or cream, and mustard or horseradish sauce, or with lightly toasted walnuts or hazelnuts.

Cooking times at 15 lb/High pressure

2–2.5 cm/¾–1 inch cubes	3–4 minutes
1 cm/½ inch slices	3 minutes

Blanch prior to freezing for 1 minute at 10 lb/Medium pressure or for 45 seconds at 15 lb/High pressure. Cook for frozen for 1–2 minutes.

CELERY

For general information about cooking Vegetables, see page 150.

Trim the base and cut off any feathery leaves and use to flavour casseroles, soups or stocks, or as a garnish.

To serve the celery as a vegetable, divide off the stems, remove any 'strings' and cut into 3.5—5 cm/1½–2 inch lengths. Place the celery in the separator basket. Put the trivet into the cooker and pour in 300 ml/½ pint water, bring to the boil, add the separator basket, fit the lid, bring to 15 lb/High pressure and cook for approximately 2–3 minutes. Reduce the pressure quickly.

To braise, remove any 'strings' from the outer stems, then cut the head into quarters, lengthways. Remove the trivet from the cooker, add 300 ml/½ pint stock and any other flavourings, bring to the boil, add the celery, fit the lid and bring to 15 lb/High pressure. Cook for about 3–4 minutes, depending on size and how soft you like the celery. Reduce the pressure quickly. Transfer the celery to a warmed serving dish. Season and thicken the liquid (see page 139), then pour over the celery.

CHICKEN

For general information about cooking Meat, see page 83. See also Casseroling, page 38, and Pot Roasting, page 110.

In a pressure cooker, the best results are achieved with whole birds and portions containing bone. Flesh that has been removed from the bone should be cut into large, bite-sized pieces.

When cooking a whole bird, the first thing to check is that it will fit easily inside the cooker with sufficient room for the steam to circulate. Make sure there are no giblets in the cavity and that the bird is well trussed. If you wish to serve stuffing with the bird, cook it separately. Frozen poultry must be allowed to thaw before cooking.

Whether or not to brown poultry in heated butter or oil before pressure cooking, depends mainly on personal preference, but it can also sometimes be governed by the recipe being followed. Joints, portions and poussins that have not been browned will require slightly longer pressure cooking time than those that have not. The times below are for birds and portions that have been quickly and lightly browned in hot oil or fat. The cooker should not be more than half full when the chicken, vegetables, if used, and liquid have been added to the cooker.

Cooking times at 15 lb/High pressure for pot roasting or casseroling

Whole chicken	5 minutes, per 450 g/1 lb
Chicken portions	5–6 minutes, depending on size
Large cubes of chicken	2–2½ minutes
Poussins	5–7 minutes

Steaming Whole chicken, poussins, chicken joints, boneless chicken breasts and cubes of chicken all cook successfully if they are placed on the trivet so they are cooked more gently by the steam from the liquid. Cooking takes very slightly longer than when chicken is cooked on the base of the cooker, but is quicker than conventional steaming.

When steaming a whole chicken, put the separator basket into the cooker before the trivet, to raise it higher from the base, and so allow sufficient water to be added for the time needed to cook the bird.

Steaming times at 15 lb/High pressure

Whole chicken, per 450 g/1 lb	about 6 minutes
Poussins, approx 350g/12 oz	about 7 minutes
Chicken portions, average	about 12 minutes
Large cubes of chicken	about 2½ minutes

Chicken with Peanut Sauce Place 4 chicken portions in a shallow, non-metallic dish. Remove the trivet from the cooker, add a little oil, and heat. Stir in 3 chopped spring onions, a large, crushed garlic clove and 5 ml/ 1 tsp ground cardamom and stir together for 2 minutes. Stir in 45 ml/3 tbsp crunchy peanut butter, 30 ml/2 tbsp tomato ketchup, 15 ml/1 tbsp lemon juice, a few drops of Tabasco sauce, freshly ground black pepper and

275 ml/9 fl oz water. If time allows, pour over 4 chicken portions and leave in a cool place for 2–3 hours, turning the chicken over occasionally. Remove chicken from peanut mixture. Bring peanut mixture to the boil in the cooker, add chicken, fit the lid and bring to 15 lb/High pressure. Cook for 5–6 minutes, depending on size. Reduce the pressure quickly. Transfer chicken to a warmed serving plate and keep warm. Boil the cooking liquid until reduced by about half. Taste and adjust the seasoning and flavourings. Pour over the chicken and garnish with sliced spring onions.

Cold Chicken with Lemon, Coriander and Cucumber Sauce Season 1.5–1.6 kg/3–3½ lb chicken inside and out. Remove the trivet from the pressure cooker, put in the thinly pared rind and juice of 2 lemons, 30 ml/2 tbsp roughly chopped fresh coriander, 2 chopped garlic cloves and 350 ml/12 fl oz chicken stock. Bring to the boil, add the chicken, spoon the liquor over the bird, then fit the lid, bring to 15 lb/High pressure and cook for 15–18 minutes, depending on size. Reduce the pressure quickly.

Meanwhile, grate ½ cucumber and squeeze out in a clean cloth to remove excess moisture. Mix with 300 ml/ ½ pint strained Greek yogurt, finely grated rind of 1 lemon, and 15 ml/1 tbsp chopped fresh coriander.

Lift the chicken from the cooker, draining it well, and leave until it is just cool enough to handle. Boil the cooking juices until reduced by about half. Pour into a basin or jug.

Strip off skin from chicken, remove the flesh from the bones, cut into large pieces and place on a shallow serving dish. Blend a couple of spoonfuls of the cooking liquor into the yogurt sauce; adjust the seasoning. Pour over the chicken, turning pieces to coat them in sauce. Chill for 2–3 hours. Garnish with lemon slices and fresh coriander.

CHICK-PEAS

For general information about cooking Pulses, see page 114.

Pour sufficient boiling water over the chick-peas to well cover them, and leave to soak for 1 hour. Drain, reserving the liquid if it is to be used for cooking the chick-peas, and make up to the required volume with water or stock.

Remove the trivet from the cooker, pour in 900 ml/ 1½ pints water, stock or the reserved soaking liquid for every 225 g/8 oz chick-peas. Do not add salt until after cooking otherwise it will toughen the chick-peas and hamper the absorption of water. Bring to the boil, add the chick-peas, stir well and return to the boil. Skim the scum from the surface, adjust the heat so the liquid is boiling but the contents of the cooker are not rising, fit the lid and, maintaining the same heat, bring to 15 lb/ High pressure. Adjust the heat so the pressure is just maintained, and cook for 15–20 minutes. Reduce the pressure slowly, and drain chick-peas. Flavour and season to taste.

Hummous Soak and cook 100 g/4 oz chick-peas in 600 ml/1 pint water in the pressure cooker, as above. Drain cooked chick-peas with reserved cooking liquor, 2 crushed garlic cloves, the juice of 1 lemon and 30 ml/ 2 tbsp olive oil. Season to taste and spoon into a bowl. Trickle a circle of olive oil over the surface and sprinkle paprika pepper and chopped mint or parsley over. Serve with pitta bread.

CHRISTMAS PUDDING

For further information on cooking puddings, see page 113. In a large bowl, stir together 100 g/4 oz self-raising flour, 100 g/4 oz fresh wholemeal breadcrumbs, 50 g/ 2 oz each muscovado and demerara sugar, 5 ml/1 tsp each mixed spice, nutmeg and a couple of good pinches of ground cloves. Rub in 50 g/2 oz chopped butter, then stir in 50 g/2 oz shredded suet. Roughly chop 1 small orange and 1 small lemon, with the skins left on. Remove the pips, then place both fruits in a blender or food processor and reduce to a course purée, leaving some pieces of peel still intact. Stir into the flour mixture with 2 lightly beaten eggs, 100 g/4 oz each sultanas, chopped raisins, grated apple, grated carrot and currants, 50 g/2 oz candied peel, 25 g/1 oz chopped walnuts or almonds, 75 ml/5 tbsp Guinness, stout (or cider or milk), 45 ml/3 tbsp sherry, port or brandy, and 30 ml/2 tbsp black treacle.

Mix until evenly blended, then cover and leave overnight in a cool place to allow the fruit to absorb some of the moisture and swell, and the flavours to mature and meld together.

Spoon into one 900 g/2 lb, or two 450 g/1 lb suitably greased basins, filling them no more than two-thirds full. Cover with a treble thickness of greaseproof paper, and pleated foil, and tie securely in place. Place one basin on the trivet, in pressure cooker containing the right amount of water (see chart). Fit the lid, without the weights, and heat until steam escapes through the vents. Adjust the heat to maintain a gentle flow of steam from the vents, and steam for the appropriate time. Fit the weights and bring the cooker to 15 lb/High pressure and cook for the required time. Reduce the pressure slowly.

Leave the pudding to cool. Do not remove the greaseproof paper cover. Store in a cool place.

Cooking times at 15 lb/High pressure

Weight of mixture	Amount of water
450 g/1 lb	1.4 litres/2¼ pints
675 g/1½ lb	1.75 litres/3 pints
900 g/2 lb	2 litres/3½ pints

Pre-steaming time	Cooking time	Reheating time
15 minutes	1½ hours	20 minutes
25 minutes	2¼ hours	30 minutes
30 minutes	2¾ hours	30 minutes

Note: A pressure cooker can be used to quickly reheat homemade or bought Christmas puddings and there is no need to pre-steam.

CHUTNEYS

Using a pressure cooker to make chutney not only cuts down the time taken, but also reduces the smell of vinegar. The closed cooker is used for the initial softening of the fruit and vegetables; the final boiling down to the required consistency is done without the lid in place.

Remove the trivet from the cooker, add the fruit, vegetables, flavourings and half the vinegar, making sure the cooker is not more than half full when all the ingredients have been added. Fit the lid, bring to 10 lb/Medium pressure and cook for about a third of the normal first boiling period, then reduce the pressure slowly.

Using a wooden spoon, stir in the sugar over a low heat until dissolved, then add remaining vinegar, and bring to the boil in the open cooker. Boil for the time specified in the recipe, until the chutney thickens. Pour into warmed, clear jars and cover with vinegar-proof closures.

Apple and Pear Chutney Peel, core and chop 675 g/ 1½ lb apples and 675 g/1½ lb cooking or under-ripe pears. Using a potato peeler, pare the rind from 1 large orange and 1 lemon, and chop finely; squeeze out juice from fruit. Put apples, pears, fruit rinds and juice into the base of the cooker, without the trivet in place, and add 350 g/12 oz chopped onions and 175 g/6 oz chopped raisins. Fit the lid and bring to 15 lb/High pressure. Cook for 8 minutes, then reduce the pressure slowly.

Remove lid, and, over a low heat, stir in 275 g/10 oz demerara sugar and a further 300 ml/½ pint white vinegar, bring to the boil and simmer in the open pan until the chutney thickens. Pour into warm, dry, clean jar. Cover, label and store in a cool, dark, dry place.

COD

For general information about cooking Fish, see page 59.

Cod is a relatively firm yet tender, flaky fish. It can be cooked both on the trivet, and on the base of the cooker, surrounded by a liquid, if attention is paid to the cooking – not pre-frying the fish, bringing liquid to the boil before adding the fish, cooking for the minimum time and timing the cooking very accurately. Cod fillet is usually thicker at one end than the other, so, to help it to cook evenly, fold the thinner end back over itself, to make a double thickness.

Cooking times at 15 lb/High pressure
On the trivet

Fillets	about 2½ minutes, depending on thickness
Steaks and cutlets	about 3 minutes

In the cooker

Fillets	about 2 minutes
Steaks and cutlets	about 2½ minutes

Cod with Tomatoes and Peppers Cook 2 sliced onions in a little oil in the cooker, stirring occasionally, until beginning to colour. Add 2 crushed garlic cloves, a sliced carrot, a sliced stick of celery and a sliced red pepper and cook over a low heat for 2–3 minutes. Add 450 g/1 lb peeled, seeded and chopped tomatoes, 10 ml/2 tsp tomato purée and 5–10 ml/1–2 tsp chopped fresh oregano. Pour in 150 ml/¼ pint each dry white wine and fish stock and bring to the boil. Add 4 cod steaks, fit the lid, bring to 15 lb/High pressure and cook for 3½ minutes. Reduce the pressure quickly.

Transfer fish to a warmed serving dish and keep warm. Boil the cooking liquid to thicken slightly. Adjust the seasoning and amount of tomato purée and oregano, if necessary, then pour over fish. Scatter stoned black olives and plenty of parsley over.

CONTAINERS

Most heatproof containers, including baking tins, casserole and soufflé dishes can be used in a pressure cooker, but only use plastic containers that can withstand temperatures up to 130°C/262°F. Using a dish that can also be used for a serving dish will save unnecessary movement of the food, time, and washing up. Check that the container will fit inside the cooker. Use a separator basket, or a foil 'lifting strap' (see page 77) for lowering containers into, and removing them from the cooker.

Containers can be placed on top of each other, providing they do not fill the base of cooker more than two-thirds of its capacity.

COOKING TIMES

The length of the cooking is determined by the size of the pieces of food, not by their quantity or volume. So, whether cooking 450 g/1 lb potatoes or 1 kg/2¼ lb, the cooking time will be the same, provided the potatoes are the same size. To avoid overcooking, unless instructed to the contrary (as when cooking pulses), bring the cooker up to pressure as quickly as possible, and immediately start the timing. As the majority of cooking times are short, it is important to be accurate in the timing. As soon as the cooking is completed, reduce the pressure.

If vegetables are to be kept warm whilst a sauce is being made, they should be cooked for slightly less time. When cooking meat, it should be remembered that the meat will continue to cook if it is kept warm whilst a sauce is being made, and that the meat should be allowed to stand for a short while before it is tested, or cut, to give the heat time to even out inside the meat.

COURGETTES

For general information about cooking Vegetables, see page 150.

For the best results when pressure cooking, use slim to medium courgettes. As they are a delicate vegetable that easily becomes watery if overcooked, it is better to cut them, after trimming, into approximately 2.5–3.5 cm/ 1–1½ inch lengths than to slice them more thinly. If liked, they can be quickly sliced after cooking. Slim ones can also be cooked whole.

Place the courgettes in the separator basket. Put the trivet into the cooker and pour in 300 ml/½ pint water, bring to the boil, add the separator basket, fit the lid, bring to 15 lb/High pressure and cook for the time given (see below). Reduce the pressure quickly.

Cooking times at 15 lb/High pressure

Medium courgettes, 3.5 cm/1½ inch lengths	about 1–1¼ minutes
Slim courgettes, whole	about 1¼–1½ minutes

COVERINGS

Ideal materials for covering foods are greaseproof paper, aluminium foil or cloth. They must be securely fitted or tied onto the container to prevent them coming loose during cooking, and so blocking the pressure cooker safety outlets.

Fitted plastic or metal lids should not be used as they prevent the steam penetrating the food. Also, they might become distorted and detach themselves during the cooking and block the safety outlets.

CURDS

Fruit curds, such as lemon curd, can be made effortlessly and quickly in a pressure cooker. Made from fruits, sometimes with the addition of other flavourings, unsalted butter, egg yolks and sugar, they have the consistency of thick honey.

Orange and Ginger Curd Finely grate the rind from 2 large oranges. Strain the juice from the oranges, and ½ a lemon into a heatproof bowl or dish that will easily fit inside the cooker. Strain in 3 egg yolks, then stir in the orange rind, 100 g/4 oz diced unsalted butter and 175 g/6 oz caster sugar.

Cover the bowl or dish with a double thickness of greaseproof paper and tie securely in place. Pour 300 ml/½ pint water into the cooker, put in the trivet and, using a 'lifting strap' (see page 77) or the separator basket, lower into the bowl or dish. Fit the lid, bring to 10 lb/High pressure and cook for 2 minutes. Reduce the pressure slowly.

Strain the curd, stir in 60 ml/4 tbsp chopped preserved ginger and pour into warmed, clean, dry jars. Cover, label and leave to cool. This preserve will keep in the refrigerator for 2–3 weeks.

Lemon Curd Make as for Orange and Ginger Curd, substituting the rind and juice of 3 lemons for the oranges and juice of ½ lemon.

D

DAMSONS

For general information about cooking Fruit, see page 62.

The pressure cooker can be used for cooking halved and stoned damsons, or whole fruit, their skins having been pricked first with a needle.

Put the damsons in a heatproof container that will fit inside the cooker, add a little water to provide juice to serve with the fruit, and a little sugar, if liked. Cover with a double thickness of greaseproof paper and tie securely in place. Put the trivet into the cooker and pour in 300 ml/½ pint water. Lower into the container, using the separator basket, or a 'lifting strap' (see page 77). Fit the lid and bring to 10 lb/Medium pressure, or 15 lb/High pressure if the cooker has only a single pressure control. Reduce the pressure immediately, and quickly.

DRIED FRUIT

Using a pressure cooker, there is no need to soak traditional, untreated dried fruits overnight.

Remove the trivet, put the fruit in the cooker, add 600 ml/1 pint liquid (water, sherry, dessert wine, fruit juice or tea) per 450 g/1 lb fruit and leave to stand for 10 minutes. Do not fill the cooker more than half-full. Bring to 15 lb/High pressure and cook for the time given (see below). Reduce the pressure slowly.

Cooking times at 15 lb/High pressure

Apricots, peaches	3 minutes
Apple rings, figs, fruit salad, pears, prunes	10 minutes

If using no-need-to-soak dried fruit, do not soak for 10 minutes, and reduce the times given above by 1 minute.

Mulled Dried Fruit Compôte Put 450 g/1 lb mixed dried fruits – stoned prunes, apricots, pears, peaches, figs – into a bowl, add a strip of lemon rind, the grated rind and juice of 1 orange, 2.5 cm/1 inch cinnamon stick and 2 cloves. Heat 150 ml/¼ pint each sweet sherry and dessert wine to just below simmering point and pour into the bowl. Cover and leave to soak for 10 minutes.

Pour the contents of the bowl into the pressure cooker, bring to 15 lb/High pressure and cook for 6–8 minutes, depending on how soft you like the fruit.

Meanwhile, peel an orange and divide into segments. Reduce the pressure slowly. Remove the cinnamon stick and cloves and serve the compôte warm or cold, with the orange segments and flaked almonds scattered over, and accompanied by whipped cream, fromage blanc or strained Greek yogurt.

DUCK

For general information about cooking Meat, see page 83, Casseroling, page 38, and Pot Roasting, page 110. Duck can be cooked successfully in the pressure cooker.

Whole Duck If cooking a whole bird, make sure that it will fit inside the cooker. Trim away excess fat, sprinkle black pepper over the skin and in the cavity, and put 2 or 3 wedges of lemon or orange and some herbs into the cavity. Remove the trivet from the cooker. Quickly brown the bird evenly in a little hot oil over a high heat, in the cooker, then drain onto absorbent kitchen paper.

Sauté some chopped vegetables, such as an onion, carrot, celery and leek, in the fat in the cooker, then drain. Pour away surplus fat. Stir 450 ml/¾ pint liquid (such as stock, wine or cider) into the cooker, add herbs or a few cloves or a cinnamon stick; bring to the boil. Return vegetables to cooker and place duck on top. Fit the lid and bring quickly to 15 lb/High pressure. Cook for 8 minutes per 450 g/1 lb. Reduce the pressure quickly.

Transfer duck and vegetables to a warmed serving dish. Remove excess fat from the surface of cooking liquid, then boil until reduced. Remove sprigs of herbs or whole spices. Purée the vegetables with the liquid, if liked, to make a sauce. Flavour with orange juice, redcurrant jelly or port. Adjust the seasoning and serve with the duck.

Duck Portions Trim away excess fat and remove skin, if liked. If leaving the skin on, brown quickly in a little hot oil in the cooker over a high heat, then drain onto absorbent kitchen paper. Treat in the same way as whole duck, but using only 300 ml/½ pint liquid, and cook for about 8 minutes, depending on the size of the portions and how well cooked you like duck.

Duck with Grape Sauce Remove the trivet from the cooker. Pour in 300 ml/½ pint white grape juice and add 225 g/8 oz halved, seedless white grapes and 2 strips of orange rind. Bring to the boil, add 4 skinned duck portions, fit the lid and bring to 15 lb/High pressure. Cook for about 8 minutes. Reduce the pressure quickly.

Transfer duck to a warmed plate and keep warm. Boil the cooking juices until reduced. Remove orange rind and skim the fat from the surface. Purée the liquid, then reheat. Season to taste, adding lemon juice, if necessary, to 'lift' the flavour, and finish, if liked, by swirling in a couple of knobs of unsalted butter. Pour around the duck and garnish with small bunches of grapes.

Note: Use Muscat grapes if they are available, and substitute 150 ml/¼ pint each veal stock and dry white wine for the grape juice.

DUMPLINGS

Dumplings can be cooked in a pressure cooker, following a special method.

As when cooking a stew or casserole by conventional methods, cook the meat and vegetables in the liquid first, then release the pressure slowly. Remove the lid and bring the stew or casserole just to the boil, add the dumplings, replace the lid, without the weights in place (or, if using an automatic cooker, with the pressure release control knob open), and simmer for 10–15 minutes until dumplings have risen and are fluffy.

Sunflower Seed Dumplings Rub 75 g/3 oz margarine into 175 g/6 oz self-raising flour, then stir in 50 g/2 oz sunflower seeds and sufficient cold water to form a not too stiff dough. Shape into 12 balls and cook at once.

E

EGGS

Egg custards, such as crème brulée and crème caramels, and dishes containing egg custard mixtures, such as bread and butter pudding, cook surprisingly well in a pressure cooker. Cover the tops of dishes with a double thickness of greaseproof paper, and tie securely in place.

Put the trivet into the cooker, pour in the required amount of water (see recipes) and bring to the boil. Lower the dish, or dishes, containing the egg custard into the cooker using the separator basket, or a 'lifting strap' (see page 77), taking care not to spill any mixture. Fit the lid and bring to 15 lb/High pressure, and cook for the time specified in the recipe. The exact shape, size, and material, of the dishes will affect the cooking times, so it may be necessary to experiment with dishes to determine precise cooking times. Always reduce the pressure slowly to prevent curdling.

Baked Egg Custard Warm 600 ml/1 pint milk with 30 ml/2 tbsp caster sugar. Lightly beat together 3 eggs and a few drops of vanilla essence, then stir in the warm, sweetened milk. Strain into a buttered 900 ml/1½ pint ovenproof dish. Sprinkle a little grated nutmeg over the top, then cover dish with a double thickness of greaseproof paper, and tie securely in place.

With the trivet in place in pressure cooker, pour in 300 ml/½ pint water. Bring to the boil, lower in the dish of custard using the separator basket or a 'lifting strap' (see page 77), fit the lid and bring quickly to 15 lb/High pressure. Cook for about 8 minutes until just set in the centre. Reduce the pressure slowly.

Lift the dish from the cooker, uncover and leave to cool. Cover and chill.

Rose Custard Use a few drops of rose water instead of vanilla essence. This is particularly good with a creamy custard (see below).

Coffee Custard Add about 10 ml/2 tsp instant coffee to the milk.

Honey Custard Sweeten the custard with clear honey instead of sugar.

For more creamy desserts, replace some of the milk by cream.

Chocolate Rum Custard Melt 50 g/2 oz chopped plain chocolate in a bowl placed over a saucepan of hot water. Remove from the heat and stir in 90 ml/6 tbsp dark rum, 30 ml/2 tbsp sugar and 2 beaten eggs. Stir in 300 ml/½ pint hot milk, then strain into 4 individual heatproof dishes placed in the separator basket. Cover each dish with a double thickness of greaseproof paper; secure in place. Cook at 15 lb/High pressure for 3 minutes. Reduce pressure slowly. Sprinkle toasted flaked almonds over the top and serve warm or cold.

Crème Caramel In a small saucepan, gently heat 150 ml/¼ pint water and 100 g/4 oz sugar, stirring with a wooden spoon, until the sugar has dissolved. Bring to the boil and keep there, without stirring, until it turns a golden brown. Pour into four warmed, individual heatproof dishes. Leave to cool.

Warm together 300 ml/½ pint milk and 150 ml/¼ pint single cream, then stir into 4 beaten egg yolks (or 3 yolks and 1 whole egg). Add a few drops of vanilla essence and 15 g/½ oz sugar. Strain over the caramel. Cover the dishes with foil, or a double thickness of greaseproof paper, and tie securely in place. Pour 300 ml/½ pint water into the pressure cooker, put in the trivet and place dishes on the trivet. Fit the lid and bring to 15 lb/High pressure and cook for 3 minutes. Reduce the pressure slowly.

Remove dishes from the cooker, uncover and leave to cool. Chill for several hours. To serve, gently ease the edge of each custard from the dish, then invert onto a plate.

Bread and Butter Pudding Generously butter 4 slices bread from a large loaf, then remove crusts. Layer bread in a buttered, heatproof container with 40 g/1½ oz mixed dried fruit, 15 ml/1 tbsp chopped mixed peel and 50 g/2 oz sugar. Beat together 2 eggs, 450 ml/¾ pint milk (or milk and cream mixed), a few drops of vanilla essence and a large pinch of ground cinnamon or nutmeg. Strain over the bread. Cover dish with a double thickness of greaseproof paper and tie securely in place.

Put the trivet into the cooker and pour in 300 ml/ ½ pint water. Lower in the container, using a separator basket or 'lifting strap' (see page 77), fit the lid, bring to 15 lb/High pressure and cook for 6 minutes. Reduce the pressure slowly.

Sprinkle a layer of brown sugar over the top of the pudding and place under a pre-heated grill until lightly browned.

ETHNIC COOKING

With the short cooking times of pressure cooking, freshly cooked ethnic dishes lack the subtle taste and individual, distinctive characters gained from the long, slow cooking that allows the flavours of a blend of spices to gradually meld and mellow together. However the flavour will improve if the dish is cooled quickly after cooking (it is best to slightly undercook it) then kept overnight before reheating to serve. Meat and poultry dishes will also benefit from marinating in the spices before cooking.

F

FENNEL

For general information about cooking Vegetables, see page 150.

Slice off the woody base, trim the stalks and cut into quarters. Cook on the trivet with 300 ml/½ pint water at 15 lb/High pressure for 2–3½ minutes, depending on size, age and how crisp you like vegetables to be. Reduce pressure quickly.

Cooked fennel is good tossed with lightly toasted flaked almonds – include some lightly seasoned, warmed cream for a luxury touch, or olive oil and freshly grated Parmesan cheese. Or, put the cooked fennel in a heatproof dish, scatter breadcrumbs mixed with freshly grated Parmesan cheese and place under a hot grill until golden and bubbling.

FIGS

The pressure cooker can be used for cooking dried figs, without first giving them an overnight soak.

Remove the trivet, put figs in the cooker, add 600 ml/ 1 pint liquid (water, sherry, dessert wine or fruit juice) per 450 g/1 lb figs and leave to stand for 10 minutes. Do not fill the cooker more than half-full. Bring to 15 lb/ High pressure and cook for 10 minutes. Reduce the pressure slowly.

Flavour the cooking liquid with orange or lemon rind, a vanilla pod or stick of cinnamon.

FISH

The main advantage of cooking fish in the pressure cooker is the reduction of the characteristic cooking smell. Cooking times for fish are not usually very long; so using a pressure cooker does not save much time.

Fish can be cooked in a liquid in the bottom of the cooker, or placed on the trivet so that it cooks in the stream produced by the liquid. This is the best method to use when cooking fragile fish, such as plaice, because it will keep its shape better. Whichever method you use, bring the liquid quickly to pressure and time the cooking accurately as fish is easily overcooked. Because the cooking is so quick, pressure cooking is more suitable for whole fish, steaks or cutlets than fillets, especially from the more delicate fish such as plaice; these are best if rolled rather than cooked flat.

Fish can be given some protection against overcooking, plus added flavour, if it is wrapped in foil or greaseproof paper (*en papillote*); in bacon (the flavour of bacon goes particularly well with trout and cod), or lettuce or cabbage leaves. Cooking times will be slightly longer if the fish is enclosed in foil or greaseproof paper – about an extra 30 seconds–1 minute for plaice fillets and trout respectively; 1 minute for steaks or cutlets, or 2 minutes for a whole fish, such as an average-sized trout or mackerel.

If enclosing fish in foil parcels, add some chopped vegetables, herbs, spices, a knob of butter or soft cheese, or some wine or vermouth, for extra flavour.

Whole Fish Always check that the number of whole fish you wish to cook will all fit comfortably into the cooker. Sprinkle inside and out with freshly ground black pepper and lemon juice, and place 2 or 3 lemon or lime wedges and some herbs in the cavities. Bring the required amount of flavoured liquid to the boil before adding the fish, whether being cooked directly in the liquid or on the trivet. Fit the lid and bring quickly to 15 lb/High pressure. Cook for the time given (see below). Reduce the pressure quickly.

Fish Fillets Should be cooked on the trivet. Season with freshly ground black pepper and lemon or lime juice, and sprinkle with fresh herbs, or spread with soft cheese, flavoured with herbs and garlic, pesto, or a stuffing mixture. Fold the fillet in half lengthways, or roll up from the narrow, tail end, skin side outermost.

Pour 300 ml/½ pint liquid into the cooker, put in the trivet and either place the fillets directly on the trivet, or lower them in using the separator basket. Fit the lid, bring to 15 lb/High pressure and cook for the time given (see chart below). Reduce the pressure quickly. Whole fish take 4–5 minutes, depending on size; fillets, about 3 minutes.

If steaming the fish on the trivet, use the liquid to make a sauce.

Cooking times at 15 lb/High pressure, depending on thickness of fish

Fillets of delicate fish:
plaice, sole, whiting, brill

flat with skin	1½ minutes
skinned	1 minute
rolled	2½ minutes

Steaks and cutlets of firmer fish:
cod, haddock, salmon

	3 minutes

Oily fish:
mackerel, herring, trout

folded fillets	2 minutes
whole	5–6 minutes

See also individual entries such as Cod, Haddock and Plaice.

FRUIT, FRESH

See individual entries such as Apples, Blackberries.

A pressure cooker is useful for quickly cooking under-ripe fruit, such as pears, as they will be ready to eat in 6–8 minutes. Pressure cooking, however, is not suitable for very ripe fruits, ripe strawberries, or raspberries. A pressure cooker also makes short work of cooking gluts of fresh fruit for freezing to serve as cooked fruit, or for making into pies, tarts, flans and crumbles, before freezing.

The length of the cooking will depend on the ripeness of the fruit, its size and how it is prepared, whether whole, halved, chopped or sliced.

Fruits in a Container This is the more gentle way of cooking fruit, and it is the one that is advised for most occasions – especially for fruits that easily overcook and collapse in a pool of watery juice, such as blackberries, blackcurrants and rhubarb.

Place the prepared fruit in a heatproof container (see page 62), and add a little water, sugar, and any flavouring. Cover with a double thickness of greaseproof paper and tie securely in place. Put the trivet into the cooker and pour in 300 ml/½ pint water and bring to the boil. Lower the container into the cooker, using the separator basket of a foil 'lifting strap' (see page 77). Fit the lid and bring to 10 lb/Medium pressure, if the cooker has a three-pressure control and 15 lb/High pressure if it has a single control, and cook for the required length of time, see individual fruits. Reduce the pressure quickly, unless directed otherwise.

Directly in the Cooker This method can be used for hard fruits, such as firm cooking pears and large quantities for puréeing. (Smaller amounts for puréeing – for example, to serve 4 – are best cooked in a container because the amount of water that must be in the cooker will make the purée too thin.) Remove the trivet, and pour in a minimum of 300 ml/½ pint water or fruit juice. Bring to the boil, add the fruit, making sure the cooker is not more than half-full. Fit the lid and bring to 15 lb/High pressure. Cook for the time required. Reduce the pressure slowly.

Strain off juice and reserve. Purée the fruit, if required. If necessary, add sufficient juice to give the right consistency. Adjust the sweetness, if necessary, if serving immediately, otherwise wait until the purée is to be used, or served, so that the most suitable type and level of sweetener can be used.

G

GAMMON
Gammon is the hind leg of a cured side of bacon, and is cooked and eaten in the same way as Bacon, see page 18.

GASKET
A faulty ring will cause loss of steam and affect cooking times, and may boil dry. Steam escaping from under the lid of the cooker during cooking could be caused by a gasket that has not been fitted properly against the inner wall of the lid, or has shrunk slightly. If the gasket is fitting snugly, remove the gasket and check it for

damage or signs of wear. If it is in good condition, when it is cold, rub with a mild cooking oil, stretch it slightly and fit it back into the cooker, the other way up to even out the wear. Do not stretch the gasket whilst hot as it may break.

If the cooker is not used for a while the gasket will harden, so rub it with a mild cooking oil before cooking. It is also a good idea to rub a new gasket with oil before fitting it into the cooker. Replace the gasket every 9–12 months or so.

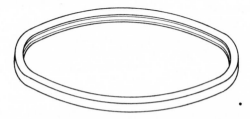

A leak that persists after the gasket has been checked or renewed may well be due to a damaged lid or cooker, so check them. If either is faulty, contact the local service agent, or the manufacturer.

GOOSEBERRIES

For general information about cooking Fruit, see page 62.

Use gooseberries that are not too soft. Wipe them if they are dirty, or likely to have been sprayed with pesticides and top and tail them, unless making a purée that is to be sieved.

Put the berries into a heatproof container that will fit inside the cooker, add a little water to provide juice to serve with the fruit, and a little sugar, if liked. Cover with a double thickness of greaseproof paper and tie securely in place.

Put the trivet into the cooker and pour in 300 ml/ ½ pint water and bring to the boil. Lower in the container, using the separator basket, or a 'lifting strap' (see page 77). Fit the lid, bring to 10 lb/Medium pressure and cook for 1–1½ minutes, or at 15 lb/High pressure if the cooker has only a single pressure control for about 1 minute, depending on firmness of the fruit.

A few drops of orange flower water sprinkled onto cooked gooseberries or added to gooseberry dishes, enhances their flavour beautifully, and elderflower blossoms, which come out in late May and June, give the berries a wonderful taste.

GRAINS

Not only are cooking times reduced but pressure cooking also does away with the overnight soaking required by some grains, such as barley.

Remove the trivet from the cooker, pour in plenty of boiling water allowing 900 ml/1½ pints to every 100 g/ 4 oz grain and bring to the boil. Add the grains, stir and bring to the boil. Adjust the heat so the liquid is boiling, but the contents of the cooker are not rising. Fit the lid and bring to 15 lb/High pressure. Over the same heat, cook for the required length of time. Reduce the pressure slowly.

As good as grains are to eat on their own, they combine easily with other ingredients and flavourings: stir in some diced cooked vegetables, such as carrot, onion, mushrooms, green and red peppers; flavour with herbs and spices; scatter over and stir-in toasted sesame or pumpkin seeds, or chopped nuts; toss with olive oil and/or lemon juice; stir in natural yogurt or serve with a flavourful sauce, such as tomato. Also try combining different grains, such as rice and barley.

See also Barley, page 19, Oats, page 89 and Wholewheat, page 156.

GREENGAGES

See Plums, page 107.

H

HADDOCK

For general information about cooking Fish, see page 59.

Haddock is a relatively firm fish, so can be cooked on the trivet, or on the base of the cooker. Haddock fillet is usually thicker at one end than the other, so, to help it cook evenly, fold the thinner end back over itself to make a double thickness.

Cooking times at 15 lb/High pressure

On the trivet

Fillets	about 2½ minutes, depending on thickness
Steaks and cutlets	about 3 minutes

In the cooker

Fillets	about 2 minutes, depending on thickness
Steaks and cutlets	about 2½ minutes

Haddock with Quick Parsley Sauce Sprinkle lemon juice and black pepper over 4 haddock steaks. Put the trivet into the cooker and pour in 300 ml/½ pint fish stock or use half stock and half medium bodied, dry white wine. Bring to the boil, add the fish, fit the lid, bring to 15 lb/High pressure and cook for about 2½ minutes. Reduce the pressure quickly. Transfer haddock to a warmed serving plate and keep warm.

Boil the cooking liquor until reduced by half. Lower the heat and stir in 150–175 g/5–6 oz full fat, soft cheese, flavoured with garlic and herbs. Heat through gently, stirring with a wooden spoon, but do not allow to boil. Stir in approximately 15 ml/1 tbsp chopped parsley. Season to taste, adding lemon juice, if necessary, to 'lift' the flavour. Garnish haddock with parsley, spoon the sauce beside it, and serve with lemon wedges.

HAKE

For general information about cooking Fish, see page 59.

Hake has fine, flaky flesh, and is somewhat lighter than cod, so is best cooked on the trivet.

Cooking times at 15 lb/High pressure

Steaks, fillets

175 g/6 oz   about 2½ minutes

HEARTS

For general information about cooking Meat, see page 83; for Pot Roasting, page 110, and Casseroling, page 38.

For best results, use small sheep's hearts, and for preference, marinade before cooking (see Meat, page 83).

Stuffed Hearts Wash 4 small sheep's hearts, remove any tubes or gristle and wash again. Marinate for about 4 hours in red wine. Drain and pat dry. Mix together 100 g/4 oz breadcrumbs, a finely chopped onion, 45 ml/3 tbsp melted butter, 10 ml/2 tsp dried mixed herbs and salt and freshly ground black pepper. Fill hearts with mixture and tie firmly into their original shape, using string. Coat hearts in 30 ml/2 tbsp seasoned flour.

Heat a little oil in the base of the pressure cooker, add the hearts and brown quickly all over. Pour in 175 ml/6 fl oz veal, chicken or vegetable stock and 150 ml/¼ pint red wine, or the marinade (or use all stock, or 325 ml/11 fl oz water) and add 1 thickly sliced onion, 2 thickly sliced carrots and 4 thickly sliced sticks of celery. Fit the lid, bring to 15 lb/High pressure and cook for about 15 minutes. Reduce the pressure quickly. Transfer hearts to a warmed serving dish. Remove vegetables from cooking liquor, then boil to lightly thicken. Either pour over the hearts immediately, or purée with the vegetables, reheat the pour around the hearts. If the vegetables are not puréed into the sauce, the can be served with the hearts, but they will be very soft.

HERRING

For general information about cooking Fish, see page 59.

Whole Herring When cooking whole, cleaned herring it will probably be necessary to remove either the head. or tail (or both) and check that the number you wish to cook will fit inside the pressure cooker, curving them slightly, if necessary. Sprinkle lemon juice and black pepper over the fish, and place some fresh herbs, such as fennel or dill, in the cavities.

Place the trivet in the cooker, pour in 300 ml/½ pint water or fish stock and bring to the boil. Arrange the fish on the trivet, fit the lid and bring to 15 lb/High pressure and cook for times given (see below). Reduce the pressure quickly.

Herring Fillets Sprinkle fillets with lemon juice and black pepper, then roll up from the tail, skin, or skinned, side outer-most, and secure each roll with a wooden cocktail stick. Enclose some herbs, or spread with mustard for extra flavour.

Bring 300 ml/½ pint of water or fish stock to the boil, place the fillet rolls, seam-sides down, on the trivet, fit the lid, bring to 15 lb/High pressure and cook for times given below. Reduce the pressure quickly.

Cooking times at 15 lb/High pressurre

Whole fish	about 3–4 minutes
Fillets, folded	about 2 minutes
Fillets, rolled	2 minutes

Soused Herrings Lightly season the flesh sides of 4 herring fillets. Roll up fillets from the tail, with the skin outer-most. Secure each roll with a wooden cocktail stick and place them, seam-sides down, on the base of the pressure cooker, without the trivet.

Add 150 ml/¼ pint vinegar, 150 ml/¼ pint water, a

thinly sliced, small onion, 6 black peppercorns, 3 all-spice berries, 1 bay leaf, 1 blade of mace, and a dried red chilli. Fit the lid, bring to 15 lb/High pressure and cook for 5 minutes then reduce the pressure quickly. Transfer the herrings to a serving dish and pour over the liquor. Leave until cold.

J

JAM

For general information about Preserves, see page 111.

Jams made using the pressure cooker for the preliminary boiling, have a very good, true fruit flavour and clear, bright colour. Using the pressure cooker also cuts down the preliminary boiling time for softening the fruit.

A cooker that has a 10 lb/Medium pressure control is needed. Remove the trivet, add the fruit and water to the cooker, making sure the cooker is no more than half-full, fit the lid and bring to 10 lb/Medium pressure. Cook for the required time (see below), then reduce the pressure slowly.

Over a low heat and using a wooden spoon, stir in the sugar until dissolved, then boil rapidly in the open cooker until setting point is reached see page 112, skimming the surface occasionally, about 5–20 minutes, depending on the type of fruit. Move the cooker from the heat, skim the scum from the surface, then pour into warm, clean jars. If the jam contains whole fruit, or large particles, leave it to stand for a few minutes until a light skin forms on the surface, then stir before pouring into the jars. Place waxed discs, wax side down, on the surface of the jam, so there is no air underneath, then cover the tops of the jars with dampened cellophane stretched taut. Secure in place with string, and label jars.

To adapt jam recipes for making in a pressure cooker, use half the given volume of water.

Cooking times at 10 lb/Medium pressure

Apples	4 minutes
Blackcurrants	3–4 minutes
Damsons, plums and other stoned fruits	4–5 minutes
Dried apricots	10 minutes
Gooseberries	3 minutes
Pears (cooking)	7 minutes

Blackcurrant Jam Remove the stalks from 900 g/2 lb blackcurrants and discard leaves. If necessary, wash the fruit carefully. Remove the trivet and put fruit into pressure cooker. Add 600 ml/1 pint water, fit the lid and bring to 10 lb/Medium pressure. Cook for 3–4 minutes then reduce the pressure slowly.

Remove the lid. Over a low heat, using a wooden spoon, stir in 1.4 kg/3 lb warmed sugar. When the sugar has dissolved increase the heat and bring the jam to the boil. Skim the surface and boil rapidly in the open cooker until setting point is reached, skimming the surface occasionally. Skim the surface a final time, and leave the jam to stand for about 10 minutes, to prevent the fruit rising to the top of the jars once potted. Stir the jam, then pour into warmed, dry, clean jars. Cover, label and store in a cool, dark place.

JELLIES

This applies to preserves, not desserts. For general information about Preserves, see page 111.

Using the pressure cooker for the preliminary boiling to soften the fruit, is particularly useful for fruits that take a long time to cook (such as hard fruits and citrus fruits), not only because the time saving is greater, but because the difference between the clarity and flavour of conventionally cooked and pressure cooked jellies is greater. Use a cooker that has a 10 lb/Medium pressure control.

For clear jellies with a good flavour, use ripe fruit that is in good condition. If it is dirty, or may have been sprayed with pesticides or herbicides, wash it gently. Remove the trivet from the cooker, put in the required fruit and water (if adapting a recipe for normal cooking, use half the amount of water), making sure the cooker is no more than half-full. Fit the lid and bring to 10 lb/Medium pressure. Cook for the times given in chart and reduce the pressure slowly.

Remove the lid. Mash the fruit, then pour, with the juice, into a jelly bag (or colander lined with a double thickness of muslin or fine cloth, such as a clean sheet or tea towel), suspended over a bowl, and leave to drip naturally. Do not squeeze or squash the fruit, otherwise the jelly will be cloudy.

Measure the juice and pour into the rinsed out cooker. Heat gently and add, as a general guide, 450 g/1 lb warmed sugar, for every 600 ml/1 pint of juice from fruits that are rich in pectin (the natural setting agent), such as cooking apples, damson, gooseberries, red and blackcurrants and citrus fruits, and 350 g/12 oz sugar for fruits with a medium-low pectin content, such as cherries, grapes, rhubarb and elderberries. Stir with a wooden spoon until the sugar has dissolved, then bring to the boil and boil until setting point has been reached (see page 112), removing the scum occasionally. (Using warmed sugar and dissolving it in the jelly before boiling it and removing the scum from the jelly all help to produce a clear jelly.) Give the jelly a final skim, then quickly pour into warmed, dry, clean, small jars or pots. Leave to set without moving. Cover and label.

Cooking times at 10 lb/Medium pressure

Apples	4 minutes
Blackcurrants	3 minutes
Citrus fruits	20 minutes
Gooseberries	3 minutes
Pears (cooking)	8 minutes
Quinces	7 minutes
Redcurrants	2 minutes
Stone fruits (damsons, plums)	4 minutes

Redcurrant Jelly Gently wash 1.4 kg/3 lb redcurrants, if necessary. Remove the trivet from the cooker, put in the fruit and 300 ml/½ pint water. Fit the lid, bring to 10 lb/Medium pressure and cook for 2 minutes. Reduce the pressure slowly, then proceed as above, adding 450 g/1 lb sugar to each 600 ml/1 pint juice.

Apple and Cranberry Jelly Roughly chop 1.4 kg/3 lb cooking apples, including the peel and cores. Put into the pressure cooker, without the trivet in place. Add 900 g/2 lb cranberries, the pared rind of 2 juicy lemons and 750 ml/1¼ pints water. Fit the lid, bring to 10 lb/Medium pressure and cook for 20 minutes. Reduce the pressure slowly. Proceed as above, using 450 g/1 lb warmed sugar to every 600 ml/1 pint juice, and adding the strained juice of 2 lemons (about 6 tbsp).

JERUSALEM ARTICHOKES

For general information about cooking Vegetables, see page 150.

Jerusalem artichokes are a knobbly root vegetable that resemble large pieces of fresh root ginger in appearance, but have a mild, slightly sweet, earthy flavour. When buying Jerusalem artichokes, choose those that are as smooth as possible, to make preparation easier and to cut down on wastage. If you do have some very knobbly ones, cook them unpeeled and scrape away the skins afterwards. Peel raw Jerusalem artichokes in the same way as potatoes, cut into large, even-sized pieces or slices, then immediately put them into water that has been acidulated with lemon juice, to prevent discoloration.

Pour 300 ml/½ pint water into the cooker, put the prepared artichokes in the separator basket or on the trivet, fit the lid and bring to 15 lb/High pressure. Cook for 4–6 minutes, depending on the age of the vegetables, personal preference and how the vegetable is to be used. Reduce the pressure quickly.

Toss with butter, or an olive, or hazelnut, oil dressing, or serve with a parsley, or mustard buttery sauce. Jerusalem artichokes go well with gammon, ham, prawns, monkfish and smoked mussels, lightly toasted nuts, and orange juice; they also make very good purées.

K

KIDNEYS

For general information about cooking Meat, see page 83.

Kidneys cook very quickly, and easily shrink and

become tough, so they are better cooked conventionally. However, for the best results in a pressure cooker, choose small kidneys and cut out the cores, but leave whole. Add the kidneys to the already boiling 300 ml/ ½ pint of liquid, or place on the trivet, fit the lid and bring rapidly to 15 lb/High pressure. Cook for a bare 2 minutes for 50 g/2 oz kidneys and just over for 75 g/ 3 oz ones. Reduce the pressure quickly. The kidneys can then be thickly sliced, if liked, to serve.

KIDNEY BEANS

For general information about cooking Pulses, see page 114.

When cooked in the pressure cooker, red kidney beans and kidney beans do not require soaking for hours. There is also no need to worry about whether they have had the necessary minimum of 10 minutes boiling to kill their toxins, as the whole of the cooking time is at a higher temperature.

Pour sufficient boiling water over the beans to well cover and leave for 1 hour. Drain beans, reserving the liquid if using it for cooking the beans, and make up to the required volume with water or stock. Remove the trivet from the cooker, add the beans and pour in 900 ml/ 1½ pints water, stock or reserved soaking liquid for each 450 g/1 lb beans, making sure the cooker is no more than half-full. Do not add salt at this point as it will toughen beans. Bring to the boil, skim the scum from the surface, adjust the heat so the water is boiling but the contents of the cooker are not rising. Fit the lid, and maintaining the same heat, bring to 15 lb/High pressure. Adjust the heat to just maintain the pressure and cook for 15 minutes. Reduce the pressure slowly. Drain the beans, flavour and season to taste.

Red Bean and Tomato Casserole Pour boiling water over 350 g/12 oz red kidney beans to well cover and leave to soak for 1 hour. Drain well. Heat a little oil in the pressure cooker, add a chopped onion, 2 crushed garlic cloves, and 2 chopped sticks of celery and cook, stirring occasionally, until softened, but not coloured. Stir in a finely chopped carrot and cook for a further 2–3 minutes. Stir in 15 ml/1 tbsp paprika pepper and cook, stirring, for 2 minutes. Drain the juice from 398 g/14 oz can of tomatoes, blend with 30 ml/2 tbsp tomato purée, then make up to 1.75 litres/3 pints with water or stock. Add the tomatoes and liquid, a coarsely chopped red pepper and 2 bay leaves and bring to the boil, then add beans.

Skim any scum from the surface, adjust the heat so the contents are boiling gently, but not rising. Fit the lid and, over the same heat, bring to 15 lb/High pressure and cook for 15 minutes. Reduce the pressure slowly.

Stir in 60 ml/4 tbsp fresh breadcrumbs and boil to evaporate surplus water and thicken the liquid. Adjust seasoning and flavourings. Transfer to a warmed serving dish, stir in 30 ml/2 tbsp chopped parsley, and swirl in 100 ml/4 fl oz soured cream, if liked.

KOHLRABI

For general information about cooking Vegetables, see page 150.

Kohlrabi looks something like a pale green turnip with leaves, on stems, growing from small ridges over its surface. The leaves and stems are removed before

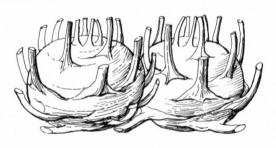

cooking. Choose young, small kohlrabi as they become tough and coarse, and require longer cooking, as they grow larger. They can easily be peeled with a vegetable knife before cooking.

Cut into quarters, or even-sized slices or pieces. Put in the separator basket, if liked. Put the trivet in the cooker, pour in 300 ml/½ pint water and bring to the boil. Add the kohlrabi, fit the lid and bring quickly to 15 lb/High pressure and, as a guide, cook 2.5 cm/1 inch cubes for about 2 minutes. Reduce the pressure quickly.

Blanch for freezing at 10 lb/Medium pressure for 1 minute and 45 seconds at 15 lb/High pressure. Cook from frozen at 15 lb/High pressure for 1 minute.

L

LAMB

For general information about cooking Meat, see page 83. See also Casseroling, page 38 and Pot Roasting, page 110.

Pressure cooking is more suitable for cooking mid and late season lamb, than young spring lamb.

Cooking times (per 450 g/1 lb) at 15 lb/High pressure

Breast, boned and rolled	12 minutes
Shoulder, boned and rolled	12 minutes
Best end	10 minutes
Chops and steaks,	
about 3 cm/1¼ inch thick	4–5 minutes
Large cubes	about 3 minutes

Oriental Lamb Stir together the finely grated rind of 1 orange and 1 small lemon, 50 ml/2 fl oz each orange and lemon juice, 15 ml/1 tbsp hoisin sauce, a crushed garlic clove and 30 ml/2 tbsp brown sugar. Peel and finely chop a 5 cm/2 inch piece of fresh root ginger and add to ingredients. Trim 4 thick lamb chump chops, place in a shallow dish and pour over the ginger mixture. Turn to coat the lamb, then leave for 1–2 hours. Drain the lamb.

Remove the trivet from the cooker, add a little oil and the lamb and quickly brown lightly on both sides. Remove. Blend 250 ml/8 fl oz veal stock into the marinade, then pour into the cooker and bring to the boil. Add the lamb, fit the lid and bring to 15 lb/High pressure. Cook for 3–4 minutes, depending on how well you like lamb cooked. Reduce the pressure quickly.

Transfer lamb to a warmed serving plate. Remove excess fat from the surface of the cooking liquid, then boil until slightly thickened and syrupy. Reduce the heat to very low and gradually whisk in 50 g/2 oz diced, unsalted butter, making sure each piece is fully incorporated before adding the next. Taste and adjust the seasonings and levels of flavouring, if necessary. Add the lamb, turn over in the sauce, then return to the plate and spoon the sauce over. Sprinkle with plenty of finely chopped parsley.

LEEKS

For general information about cooking Vegetables, see page 150.

Trim away the root ends and top, green leaves. Very slim leeks can be cooked whole, or sliced. Cut medium leeks (about 2.5 cm/1 inch in diameter), into 1–2 cm/½–¾ inch slices, halve larger ones lengthways, place cut-sides down, and cut into slices.

Put sliced leeks in the separator basket; whole ones can be cooked on the trivet or in the basket. Put the trivit in the cooker, pour in 300 ml/½ pint water and bring to the boil. Add the leeks, fit the lid and bring quickly to 15 lb/High pressure. Cook for the required time, then reduce the pressure quickly.

Cooking times at 15 lb/High pressure

Slim leeks, sliced	1 minute
Slim leeks, whole	about 2 minutes
Medium leeks, cut in 2 cm/¾ inch slices	2 minutes
Large leeks, halved and sliced lengthways	2 minutes

Blanch 2 cm/¾ inch sliced leeks for freezing for 45 seconds at 10 lb/Medium pressure, or about 30 seconds at 15 lb/High pressure. To cook from frozen, just bring to 15 lb/High pressure.

LENTILS

For general information about cooking Pulses, see page 114.

Lentils do not need to be soaked, simply remove the trivet from the cooker, add the lentils and pour in 900 ml/ 1½ pints water for each 450 g/1 lb lentils, making sure the cooker is no more than half-full. Do not add salt at this point as it will toughen the lentils. Bring to the boil, skim the scum from the surface, adjust the heat so the water is boiling but the contents of the cooker are not rising. Fit the lid, and, maintaining the same heat, bring to 15 lb/High pressure. Adjust the heat to just maintain the pressure and cook red lentils for about 3 minutes and green, brown or Continental lentils for 12–15 minutes. Reduce the pressure slowly. Drain well, flavour and season to taste.

'Lifting strap' A 'lifting strap' makes it easy to lower a container into, and to lift it out of, the pressure cooker.

Make it from a thickly folded strip of aluminium foil that is long enough to pass beneath the container with sufficient protruding on each side to enable the ends to be grasped firmly.

LIQUID

The vast majority of pressure cookers must always contain at least 300 ml/½ pint liquid when the cooker is brought to pressure, but small models can operate with less; always check with the cooker's instruction booklet. Fat and oil do not count as liquids as they do not produce the necessary steam. The amount of liquid depends on the type of recipe and the cooking time, not the amount of food. Because there is little evaporation, about 25–33% less liquid is used than in similar conventionally cooked recipes. To calculate, roughly, the amount of liquid that should be used, to allow 150 ml/ ¼ pint for every 15 minutes, or part, of pressure cooking time, plus 150 ml/¼ pint: for example, if the cooking time is 45 minutes, add 600 ml/1 pint liquid.

LIVER

Liver is sensitive to heat and will quickly shrink and toughen when cooked in the pressure cooker. Cook lambs' or calves' liver in 50–75 g/2–3 oz pieces and, if liked, slice before serving.

Add the liver to the cooker when 300 ml/½ pint liquid has come to the boil, fit the lid and bring quickly to 15 lb/High pressure. Cook for about 2 minutes. Reduce the pressure quickly.

Cooking chicken livers in the pressure cooker is not successful.

M

MACARONI

For general information about cooking Dried Pasta, see page 94.

Remove the trivet from the cooker, pour in 900 ml/ 1½ pints water for every 225 g/8 oz macaroni, bring to the boil and quickly add the macaroni. Stir, return to the boil, adjust the heat so the water is gently boiling and the contents of the cooker are not rising, fit the lid and, maintaining the same heat, bring to 15 lb/High pressure. Adjust the heat so the pressure is just maintained, and cook for about 2–3 minutes. Reduce the pressure slowly. Drain the macaroni. Season and flavour to taste.

If cooking macaroni at the same time as other foods, put the pasta into a large, wide, deep heatproof container that will fit inside the cooker, and add 15 ml/ 1 tbsp of oil to help prevent the pasta clumping together; add salt. Cover with plenty of boiling water. Stir with a fork, cover with foil or a double thickness of greaseproof paper, and secure in place with string.

Using a 'lifting strap' (see page 77), or the separator basket if it is large enough to take the container, lower the container into the cooker, fit the lid and bring to 15 lb/High pressure. Cook for about 5–6 minutes. Reduce the pressure slowly, even if the pressure is usually reduced quickly when cooking with other foods in the cooker. Strain the pasta as normal.

A change from macaroni cheese, that is much quicker to make and just as delicious to eat, can be made by tossing the cooked, drained macaroni with 100 g/4 oz broken up ricotta, or curd cheese, some freshly grated Parmesan, 7.5 ml/1½ tsp chopped fresh sage, or 5 ml/ 1 tsp dried sage, freshly ground black pepper and, if liked, 100 g/4 oz diced cooked ham.

MACKEREL

For general information about cooking Fish, see page 59.

Whole Mackerel When cooking whole, cleaned mackerel it will probably be necessary to remove either the head and tail, or both, and check that the number you wish to cook will fit inside the pressure cooker, curving them slightly, if necessary. Sprinkle lemon juice and black pepper over the fish, and place some fresh herbs, such as fennel and dill, in the cavities.

Place the trivet in the cooker, pour in 300 ml/½ pint water or fish stock and bring to the boil. Arrange the fish on the trivet, fit the lid on the cooker and bring to 15 lb/High pressure and cook for times given in chart. Reduce the pressure quickly.

Mackerel Fillets Sprinkle fillets with lemon juice and black pepper, then roll up from the tail, skin, or skinned, side outermost, and secure each roll with a wooden cocktail stick. Enclose some herbs for extra flavour. Bring 300 ml/½ pint water or fish stock to the boil, place the fillet rolls, seam-sides down, on the trivet and bring to 15 lb/High pressure and cook for times given in chart. Reduce the pressure quickly.

Mackerel, whether whole or filleted, can also be cooked in foil or greaseproof parcels with some chopped vegetables, herbs, spices, or some wine or cider added. Add 2 minutes to the cooking time for whole fish and about 1 minute for fillets. Always add the fish to the cooker after bringing the liquid to the boil. Fit the lid, bring quickly to 15 lb/High pressure and cook for times given in chart. Reduce the pressure quickly.

Cooking times at 15 lb/High pressure

Whole fish	about 4 minutes, depending on size
Whole fish, stuffed	5–6 minutes,
Fillets, folded	2 minutes
Fillets, rolled	2½ minutes

Apple Stuffed Mackerel Remove heads and tails from 4 mackerel, and trim off fins. Place each fish, skin-sides uppermost, on the work surface, with the sides of the fish spread outwards. With your thumbs, press along the backbone to loosen it. Turn the fish over and gently ease away the backbone and side bones; check the flesh for stray bones. Sprinkle a little black pepper and lemon juice inside the fish, and over the skin. Mix together 2 grated crisp, well-flavoured eating apples, a small, finely chopped onion, a little freshly chopped mint and season lightly. Bind with 15–30 ml/1–2 tbsp melted, unsalted butter. Divide between the fish and place each one on a piece of foil large enough to enclose it completely. Fold up the sides of the foil and pour a couple of spoonfuls of wine over each fish, if liked. Fold the foil loosely over the fish and secure the seams tightly.

Place in the separator basket, if a suitable size. Place the trivet in the cooker, pour in 300 ml/½ pint fish stock, or water and bring to the boil. Either lay the mackerel on the trivet, or lower in the separator basket, fit the lid and bring quickly to 15 lb/High pressure. Cook for about 6 minutes. Reduce the pressure quickly.

Either transfer fish to a warmed serving plate, spoon the cooking juices over and garnish with lemon wedges and parsley, or serve the fish in their parcels.

MARROW

Marrow is a watery vegetable with a fragile structure, so it is better to cook it by conventional methods.

MARMALADE

For general information about Preserves, see page 111.

Marmalade is a preserve made from citrus fruits, either singly or combined, and sometimes with additional flavourings, such as ginger or whisky. As with other preserves, the first stage of making marmalade is to boil the fruit without the sugar, to extract the pectin and soften the peel; once the sugar had been added, the peel will not soften further. This takes longer conventionally than when making jams and jellies – normally at least 1 hour, sometimes as long as 2–3 hours. However, using a pressure cooker reduces the time to about 15 minutes.

The fruit should be washed and scrubbed well. The peel can be sliced thickly or thinly to suit personal preference, but all the peel for a batch should be the same thickness. As the membranes, pulp, pith and pips all contain pectin, which makes the marmalade set, they should be tied in a muslin bag, with a long piece of string that can be tied to the handle of the pan so it will dangle in the marmalade during the first boiling and can easily be removed when necessary. Squeeze the bag hard to extract as much juice from it as possible, letting it flow back into the pan. Half of the water stated in a recipe is used for the first boiling, the rest is added with the sugar.

Pressure cook at 10 lb/Medium pressure, and reduce the pressure slowly. Stir in the warmed sugar and remaining water, and boil rapidly in the open cooker until setting point is reached. Over-boiling will darken the marmalade. Remove pan from heat, skim the scum from the surface and leave the marmalade to cool slightly for 10–15 minutes, then stir to distribute the peel. Ladle into warmed, clear jars; cover, cool and label. Store in a cool, dry, dark place.

When adapting marmalade recipes, cooked conventionally, use half the stated amount of water, adding half

of this for the first boiling, the other half with the sugar.
Grapefruit and Whisky Marmalade Wash 900 g/2 lb
(approximately 3) grapefruit, pare off the rinds using a
sharp knife and cut into thin strips. Remove pith and
pips from grapefruit and tie in a muslin bag with the
pips from 2 lemons. Place the muslin bag in the cooker
with grapefruit rind, lemon rind and juice, 900 ml/
1½ pints water. Fit the lid and bring to 15 lb/High
pressure and cook for 10–12 minutes. Reduce the
pressure quickly.

Remove the muslin bag and squeeze the bag over
cooked fruit to collect as much juice and pectin as
possible, then discard the bag. Return the open pressure
cooker to a low heat, add 1.75 kg/4 lb warmed
preserving or granulated sugar, and stir, using a wooden
spoon, until the sugar has dissolved. Boil rapidly until
setting point is reached. Remove from the heat, remove
any scum, using a slotted spoon, then stir in 90 ml/
6 tbsp Scotch whisky. Skim and allow to stand for 10–15
minutes, then stir to distribute the peel. Ladle into
warmed, dry jars; cover and label. Store in a cool, dry,
dark place. Makes about 2.75 kg/6 lb.

MEAT

See also individual types of meat, Casseroling, page 38
and Pot Roasting, page 110.

Whilst pressure cooking is more suitable for everyday,
cheaper cuts of meat, than expensive ones, it is not
necessarily the best way of cooking them to produce
tender, tasty dishes – or of cooking really tough cuts.
Although the atmosphere inside the pressure cooker is
moist, which has a tenderizing effect on part of the
structure of the meat, the height of the temperature
causes the meat fibres to shrink, and toughen, and it not
only loses its own flavour, but the capacity to absorb
others. The longer the cooking continues, the tougher
the meat becomes. So, even though the pieces of meat

may fall apart, they will be chewy to eat.

The secret of cooking meat in the pressure cooker is to use the right combination of cut, size of piece and cooking time. As well as following a few guidelines. Marinating the meat, especially tougher cuts, and beef in particular, in wine, cider, beer, citrus juice or plain yogurt, herbs and flavourings, before cooking will benefit both the flavour and texture. Cut meat for casseroling into large 3 cm/1¼ inch cubes, or slices about 2.5–3 cm/1–1¼ inch thick and trim away excess fat and gristle. If meat is coated in flour before cooking, the consistency of the liquid will have to be checked before the cooker lid is fitted to make sure that it is sufficiently thin. The base of the cooker must never be more than half-full when all the ingredients have been added.

Specified cooking times for meat should only be taken as a guide because the quality of the meat, the proportion of fat to lean, the age of the animal when it was slaughtered, the exact size of the piece of meat, its temperature immediately before cooking, as well as personal preference, all have a bearing. All the timings in this book are for meat starting at room temperature. Reduce the pressure quickly at the end of the cooking time, unless a recipe specifically states otherwise.

Cooking Meat from Frozen Meat that has been cut into slices or cubes can be cooked from frozen in a pressure cooker. Follow the normal method for cooking meat, and allow an additional 2 minutes or so cooking.

MILK

When milk is used as all, or part of, the cooking liquid, the pressure must be reduced slowly after cooking, otherwise the sudden drop in pressure will cause the milk to curdle.

The addition of a knob of butter, preferably unsalted, tames the tendency of the milk to froth and boil up, and when making milk puddings, helps to prevent 'catching' on the bottom of the cooker.

See Rice Pudding, page 122, and Tapioca Pudding, page 139.

MINCED MEAT

For general information about cooking Meat, see page 83.

Use good quality, lean mince. As the individual pieces of meat are small, they quickly overcook, so keep the cooking time brief to avoid toughness. If the mince is browned before cooking (which will improve the colour and flavour but not 'seal in' its natural juices), do it quickly and briefly over a high heat.

Thicken the cooking liquid after cooking. The most usual way of doing this is to stir into the cooked mince, plain flour blended with a little cold water, then stirring the mince until it boils and thickens.

Frozen mince should be allowed to partially thaw so that it can be separated into smallish lumps, then cooked as for normal mince.

Savoury Mince In the base of the cooker, sauté a chopped onion, a crushed garlic clove, 2 chopped bacon rashers and 2 chopped carrots until lightly browned. Stir in about 175 g/6 oz diced mushrooms and cook, stirring, for 2–3 minutes. Using a slotted spoon, transfer to absorbent kitchen paper to drain. Heat a little oil in the base of the cooker until really hot, add 575–675g/1¼–1½ lb minced lean beef, and cook quickly until lightly browned. Transfer to absorbent kitchen paper to drain and pour excess fat from the cooker, but leave behind the sediment.

Stir 300 ml/½ pint veal or vegetable stock into the sediment to dislodge it, then return all the ingredients to the cooker with 15 ml/1 tbsp tomato purée, 5 ml/1 tsp chopped fresh thyme, or a large pinch of dried thyme, or a dash or two of Worcestershire sauce. Fit the lid, bring to 15 lb/High pressure and cook for 3 minutes. Reduce the pressure quickly. Open the cooker and remove from heat.

Blend 15 ml/1 tbsp plain flour with a little stock or water, stir into the mince, bring to the boil, stirring, and simmer for 2 minutes. Adjust the seasoning and flavourings.

Meat Loaf Using a fork, mix together 675 g/1½ lb lean minced beef, 65 g/2½ oz fine, fresh breadcrumbs, 1 crushed garlic clove, 1 finely chopped stick of celery, 1 small, finely chopped onion, 60 ml/4 tbsp tomato ketchup, 10 ml/2 tsp Worcestershire sauce, 2.5 ml/½ tsp dried thyme, 2 beaten, medium eggs and salt and freshly ground black pepper. Transfer to a loaf tin, making sure that it is evenly filled. Cover the tin with foil or a double thickness of greaseproof paper and tie securely in place.

Put the trivet into the cooker, pour in 450 ml/¾ pint water and bring to the boil. Using a 'lifting strap' (see page 77), or the separator basket, lower the tin into place. Fit the lid, bring quickly to 15 lb/High pressure and cook for 20 minutes. Reduce the pressure quickly. Remove tin from the cooker and allow to stand for a few minutes before unmoulding.

MONKFISH

For general information about cooking Fish, see page 59.

Cooking times at 15 lb/High pressure

Steaks,
    cut across the bone   about 2½ minutes
Fillets,
    cut into large chunks   2 minutes

Monkfish and Fennel Blanquette Melt a good knob of unsalted butter in pressure cooker, stir in a small to medium fennel bulb, cut in half, and a crushed garlic clove and coat with the butter. Stir in 150 ml/¼ pint medium bodied, dry white wine, 60 ml/4 tbsp dry white vermouth and 100 ml/4 fl oz fish stock, or water. Bring to the boil, add 4 monkfish steaks (cut across the bone), fit the lid, bring to 15 lb/High pressure and cook for 2½ minutes. Reduce the pressure quickly.

Remove fish and keep warm. Lift fennel from cooking liquid, then boil liquid until reduced to about 150 ml/¼ pint. Meanwhile, slice the fennel and keep warm with the fish. Lower the heat beneath the cooker and stir in about 100–150 ml/4 fl oz/¼ pint strained Greek yogurt, to give a thick, white sauce. Return the monkfish and fennel to the sauce, and stir to coat. Serve sprinkled with the chopped feathery fronds from the fennel.

MUSHROOMS

If no other means of cooking is available, mushrooms can be cooked in the pressure cooker. Place caps, dome-sides uppermost in separator basket. Bring 300 ml/ ½ pint liquid to the boil in the cooker, add mushrooms in separator basket, fit the lid and cook at 15 lb/High pressure for 2–3 minutes, depending on size: cook diced or sliced mushrooms for about 1 minute. Reduce the pressure quickly. The mushrooms will have a good mushroom flavour but caps, in particular, are a little chewy. (Mushrooms that are to be included in dishes are perfectly satisfactory.)

N

NOODLES

Fettucine and tagliatelle for example. For general information about cooking Pasta, see page 94.

In the cooker Remove the trivet from the cooker, pour in 2 litres/3½ pints salted water for every 225 g/8 oz dried noodles and bring to the boil. Add the noodles, stir and bring to the boil. Adjust the heat so the water is boiling but the contents of the cooker are not rising, fit the lid and, over the same heat, bring to 15 lb/High pressure. Cook for 1–2 minutes, depending on thickness. Reduce the pressure slowly.

Drain the noodles and toss with olive oil or melted, unsalted butter, freshly grated Parmesan cheese, chopped parsley or torn basil leaves, and freshly ground black pepper.

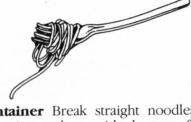

In a container Break straight noodles into shorter lengths. Put into a deep, wide, heatproof container that will fit inside the cooker. Pour on plenty of boiling salted water, add 15 ml/1 tbsp oil to help prevent the noodles clumping together, stir, then cover the container with a double thickness of greaseproof paper. Tie securely in place. Using a 'lifting strap' (see page 77), or the separator basket, lower container into the cooker containing 300 ml/½ pint boiling water. Fit the lid and bring to 15 lb/High pressure. Cook for 3½–4 minutes. Reduce the pressure slowly. Drain the noodles and flavour as above.

O

OATS

For general information about cooking Grains, see page 64.

Oat Groats Remove the trivet from the cooker, pour in 1.1 litres/2 pints water per 175 g/6 oz oats, and bring to the boil. Stir in oats, making sure the cooker is no more than half-full, adjust the heat so the contents of the cooker are boiling gently but not rising in the cooker, fit the lid and, maintaining the same heat, bring to 15 lb/High pressure, adjust the heat to just maintain the pressure and cook for 6–8 minutes. Reduce the pressure slowly.

Rolled or Porridge Oats; Coarse and Medium Oatmeal Remove the trivet from the cooker, pour in 600 ml/1 pint liquid for every 100 g/4 oz oats, if making porridge; 900 ml/1½ pints, or according to the recipe, for other dishes, and bring to the boil. Stir in the oats, making sure the cooker is no more than half-full, adjust the heat so the contents of the cooker are boiling gently, but not rising in the cooker. Fit the lid and, maintaining the same heat, bring to 15 lb/High pressure, adjust the heat to just maintain the pressure and cook rolled or porridge oats for about 1 minute; medium oatmeal for about 6–7 minutes; 15 minutes for coarse oatmeal. Reduce the pressure slowly otherwise contents of the cooker may spurt through the vents.

Wash the cooker lid carefully after use, to make sure the vents are not blocked.

ONIONS

For general information about cooking Vegetables, see page 150.

Cooking onions in a pressure cooker not only reduces their cooking time, but also their tell-tale cooking smell. The flavour of pressure-cooked onions, is closer to that of raw or boiled, onions than fried, or baked, ones.

Cook sliced or diced onions in the separator basket; whole or stuffed ones either in the separator basket or on the trivet. Add to the cooker when 300 ml/½ pint liquid has been brought to the boil, fit the lid and cook at 15 lb/High pressure for times given in chart. Reduce the pressure quickly.

Cooking times at 15 lb/High pressure

Sliced or diced onions	2 minutes
Whole onions	about 4 minutes, according to size
Stuffed onions	2 minutes, pre-cook; about 2–3 minutes, after stuffing

Stuffed Onions Cut a small slice from the top of 4 peeled onions, then stand onions on the trivet, in the cooker, and pour in 300 ml/½ pint water. Fit the lid, bring to 15 lb/High pressure and cook for 2 minutes. Reduce the pressure quickly.

When the onions are cool enough to handle, lift them from the cooker and, using a teaspoon, carefully scoop out centres, leaving a thin shell. Chop centres finely and cook in the base of the open cooker with a crushed garlic clove and 2 skinned and chopped tomatoes until almost all of the liquid has evaporated. Add 25 g/1 oz finely diced cooked ham, a pinch of chopped thyme or tarragon and freshly ground black pepper. Stand each onion on a piece of greaseproof paper or foil on the trivet and divide the filling between them. Fit the lid, bring to 15 lb/High pressure and cook for 2 minutes. Reduce the pressure quickly.

Carefully transfer the onions to a heatproof dish,

standing them upright. Sprinkle a little finely grated cheese over the tops and place under a hot grill until golden and bubbling.

Onion Sauce Roughly purée cooked, chopped onion with a little cream or fromage blanc, then transfer to a small saucepan and add a flavouring, such as freshly grated nutmeg, chopped fresh thyme, or sage, or green peppercorns, and heat through. If using cream, boil until lightly thickened, but if using fromage blanc, do not allow to boil.

ONE POT COOKING

By making use of the trivet, separator basket and dividers, complete meals can be cooked in the pressure cooker at one time, saving fuel, and cost. This ability is of particular value when cooking facilities are restricted, as when camping.

All the foods can be cooked from scratch at the same time, if they all require the same length of cooking, but if one, or some, require less time than others, they can be added part of the way through the cooking. If this is done, give the longer-cooking foods slightly less cooking time than normal as they will continue to cook whilst the pressure is being reduced and restored again. Deduct the cooking time of the quicker cooking foods from that of the longer cooking ones, then reduce the pressure in the cooker at this point. Add the shorter cooking items, replace the lid, bring to pressure and complete the cooking.

An exception to the rule is vegetables, unless you intend to purée the longer cooking ones, because their cooking times need to be precisely controlled to avoid overcooking, particularly of their outer surfaces. If you wish to cook a number of vegetables at the same time, choose ones that have similar cooking times, or cut them to appropriate sizes. See Vegetables, page 150.

Chicken with Mixed Vegetables Pour 300 ml/½ pint chicken stock into the cooker, add a finely chopped onion, 100 g/4 oz sliced button mushrooms and a sprig of tarragon. Bring to the boil, add 4 chicken breast portions, then quickly lay the trivet on top and place on it 450 g/1 lb prepared small, new potatoes (or quartered large ones), and 225 g/8 oz small whole carrots (or halved or quartered larger ones). Immediately lower in the separator basket containing 225 g/8 oz Brussels sprouts. Fit the lid and bring to 15 lb/High pressure. Cook for 4 minutes. Reduce the pressure quickly.

Transfer vegetables and chicken to a warmed serving dish and sprinkle with a little salt. Add 75 ml/5 tbsp medium bodied, dry white wine to the cooker and boil the liquid, uncovered, until reduced by almost half. Lower the heat and stir in approximately 15 ml/1 tbsp tomato purée to taste. Add freshly ground black pepper, and salt, if necessary, and pour over chicken.

OXTAIL

For general information about cooking Meat, see page 83. Also, Pot Roasting, page 110, and Casseroling, page 38.

Oxtail is a comparatively cheap, yet tough cut of meat that benefits from marinating for 4–8 hours in red wine, cider or beer.

Oxtail Stew Marinate about 900 g/2 lb well-trimmed, chopped oxtail in red wine for 4–8 hours, if time allows. Drain and pat dry. Fry a chopped onion and a chopped rasher of bacon in oil in the base of the cooker, stirring occasionally, until onion has softened, then transfer to absorbent kitchen paper. Toss oxtail in seasoned flour, add to cooker and cook, turning over occasionally, until evenly browned. Transfer to absorbent kitchen paper.

Pour off excess fat from cooker and stir in 225 g/8 oz thickly sliced carrots; cook, stirring frequently, until beginning to colour, then stir in 325 ml/11 fl oz veal stock, or 200 ml/7 fl oz stock and 150 ml/¼ pint red wine, or water, 20–25 ml/4–5 tsp tomato purée, a stick of chopped celery, and a bouquet garni. Return the oxtail, onion and bacon to the cooker, fit the lid and bring to 15 lb/High pressure. Cook for 20–25 minutes, then reduce the pressure slowly.

Taste the cooking liquor, and adjust the seasonings; if liked. Boil to thicken and concentrate the flavours. Skim the fat from the surface of the liquid. Sprinkle chopped parsley over to garnish.

P

PARSNIPS

For general notes about cooking Vegetables, see page 150.

Trim the base of parsnips and slice off tops. Cut to the required size. Place the trivet in the pressure cooker and add 300 ml/½ pint water. Put quartered parsnips on the trivet or cubed and sliced ones in the separator basket. Fit the lid and cook at 15 lb/High pressure for time given in chart. Reduce the pressure quickly. Toss with butter and orange rind, or grated fresh root ginger.

Cooking times at 15 lb/High pressure

Quarters	about 4 minutes, depending on age and size
Slices (2.5 cm/1 inch)	about 2–2½ minutes
Cubes (2.5 cm/1 inch)	about 2 minutes

When blanching prior to freezing, cook for 1 minute at 10 lb/Medium pressure or 45 seconds at 15 lb/High pressure. Cook from frozen for 1–2½ minutes, according to size, at 15 lb/High pressure.

PARTRIDGE

For general information about cooking Meat, see page 83.

To develop the flavour and soften the flesh of partridge, hang the birds by their necks for 5–8 days. Pluck and draw them and marinate in wine, herbs and spices, if liked. Cook at 15 lb/High pressure for 6½–7½ minutes (depending on how well you like the flesh cooked) for birds between 350–425 g/12–15 oz in weight, if not pre-browned, but if browned first, reduce the time by 2–3 minutes.

PASTA

Pasta needs to be cooked in plenty of water if it is to swell, so remove the trivet from the base of the cooker, and add 1.75 litres/3 pints water for every 225 g/8 oz pasta, and a pinch of salt and bring to the boil. Add the pasta, stir and check that the cooker is no more than half-full as the water has a tendency to froth and boil up. Adjust the heat so the water is boiling, but the contents of the cooker are not rising, fit the lid and bring to 15 lb/High pressure over the same heat (the steam should just be escaping gently) and cook according to type. Reduce the pressure slowly. Strain well.

If pasta is to be served with other foods that are being cooked in the pressure cooker, some can be cooked at the same time in a suitably large, wide, deep heatproof container (see page 94) that will fit inside the cooker. A large separator basket, lined with foil is only large enough for small quantities, but, because of the space that pasta occupies and the volume of water that is required, about 175 g/6 oz will be the maximum. The container must also be able to stand level in the cooker.

Put pasta into container and add 15 ml/1 tbsp of oil to help prevent the pasta clumping together, and salt. Cover with plenty of boiling water. Stir with a fork, cover with foil or a double thickness of greaseproof paper, and secure in place with string. Using a 'lifting strap' (see page 77), or the separator basket if the dish will fit inside it, lower the container into the cooker, fit the lid and bring to 15 lb/High pressure. Cook for about double the normal pressure cooking time. Reduce the pressure slowly, even if the pressure is usually reduced quickly when cooking with other foods in the cooker. Strain the pasta as normal.

See also types of pasta such as Macaroni, page 79 and Spaghetti, page 125.

PASTRY

Suet pastry is the only type that can be cooked successfully in a pressure cooker as it is actually at its best when cooked in a moist atmosphere.

Suet pastry is used for many favourite 'old-fashioned' puddings, such as Jam Roly Poly, steamed fruit puddings and Steak and Kidney Pudding.

PÂTÉ

The pressure cooker can be used to reduce the cooking time of meat pâtés. Traditionally pâtés are cooked in loaf tins, but the size of tin that will fit inside the cooker will limit the size of pâté you can make. If you want to make a larger quantity, divide it between two, or more, tins. Always cover the top of the container with a double thickness of greaseproof paper and tie securely in place. Place the container on the trivet and make sure there is sufficient water in the cooker – 300 ml/½ pint for the first 15 minutes, plus 150 ml/¼ pint for each subsequent 15 minute period. Fit the lid and cook at 15 lb/High pressure for a third of the conventional cooking time.

Pork and Chicken Liver Pâté Stretch 4 rashers of streaky bacon with the back of a knife, then use to line a 450 g/1 lb loaf tin. Finely mince 350 g/12 oz lean belly pork, 225 g/8 oz chicken livers, 1 chopped onion and a clove of garlic. Mix in 1 beaten egg, 60 ml/4 tbsp breadcrumbs, a good pinch of dried mixed herbs, 30 ml/2 tbsp brandy and seasonings. Spoon into the bacon-lined tin, packing evenly. Cover with a double thickness of greaseproof paper. Place the trivet in the cooker and pour in 450 ml/¾ pint water and 5 ml/1 tsp vinegar or lemon juice. Using a 'lifting strap' (see page 77) or the separator basket, lower loaf tin into cooker.

Fit the lid and bring to 15 lb/High pressure. Cook for 25 minutes, then reduce the pressure slowly. Lift loaf tin from cooker. Replace the greaseproof paper with a fresh piece, place weights evenly over the surface and leave to cool. Place in the refrigerator for about 8 hours, with the weights still in place. Return to room temperature about 30 minutes before unmoulding and serving.

PEACHES

For general information about cooking Fruit, see page 61.

Use the pressure cooker for peaches that are firm. Halve and stone them and either place in the separator basket, or in a heatproof container, preferably in a single layer. Sprinkle with a little sugar and add any flavouring, such as crushed cardamom seeds or orange flower water, then tie over the container a double thickness of greaseproof paper. Put the trivet in the cooker, pour in 300 ml/½ pint water and bring to the boil. Add the fruit in the separator basket or use a 'lifting strap' (see page 77) to lower in the container. Fit the lid and bring to 10 lb/Medium pressure, or 15 lb/High pressure if the cooker has only one pressure control. Cook for time given in chart. Reduce the pressure quickly. Sweeten and flavour, to taste, or use as required.

Cooking times at 15 lb/High pressure
In separator basket   about 1 minute
In a container   2 minutes

Cooking times at 10 lb/Medium pressure
In separator basket   1½–2 minutes
In separator basket   3–4 minutes

Stuffed Peaches Cut 4 firm peaches into halves and remove stones. Place, cut sides uppermost, in a shallow, heatproof dish. Pour around the peaches about 150 ml/ ¼ pint fruity, dry white wine, and add 5–10 ml/1–2 tsp clear honey. Mix together 150 g/5 oz sieved cottage cheese, 50 g/2 oz sieved soft cheese, 2–3 drops of orange flower water, and 6–8 crushed small macaroons. Sweeten to taste with about 40 g/1½ oz caster sugar. Divide between cavities in peaches, cover dish with a double thickness of greaseproof paper and tie securely in place.

Pour 300 ml/½ pint water into the cooker and put in the trivet; bring to the boil. Using a 'lifting strap' (see page 77), or the separator basket, lower in the dish. Fit the lid and bring to 10 lb/Medium pressure, or 15 lb/ High pressure. Cook for 1½–2½ minutes, and 1–2 minutes respectively. Reduce the pressure quickly.

Adjust the sweetness of cooking juices and add a little lemon juice, if necessary. Scatter toasted flaked almonds over peaches. Serve warm, or leave to cool in the cooking juice, accompanied by custard, cream, etc.

PEARS

For general information about cooking Fruit, see page 61.

Choose firm pears for cooking in the pressure cooker. They can be cooked whole, halved and cored, or sliced. Sliced pears can be cooked in a heatproof, covered container; in the separator basket or on the trivet. Whole and halved pears can be cooked in a container (and should be if on the soft side otherwise they may disintegrate); on the trivet; in the separator basket, or the base of the cooker – this is the normal method for very firm or under-ripe pears. The cooking liquid can be water, red or white wine, cider, apple or orange juice, plus added flavourings such as cloves, a vanilla pod, toasted crushed cardamom seeds or orange rind.

If cooking in a heatproof container, place the pears (preferably in a single layer) in container and sprinkle with a little sugar and add any flavouring, such as the seeds from a vanilla pod, chopped preserved or grated fresh ginger, or ground cinnamon, then tie over the container a double thickness of greaseproof paper.

Whichever method is used, bring 300 ml/½ pint liquid to the boil before adding the pears. Add the fruit, fit the lid and bring to 10 lb/Medium pressure, or 15 lb/High pressure if the cooker has only one pressure control. Cook for time given in chart. Reduce pressure quickly. Sweeten and flavour, to taste, or use as required.

Cooking times at 15 lb/High pressure

Halved, under ripe
In separator basket	about 4–5 minutes
In a container	6–8 minutes

Halved ripe, but not too soft
In separator basket	about 1½–2 minutes
In a container	3 minutes

Sliced
In separator basket	about 1 minute
In a container	2 minutes

Cooking times at 10 lb/Medium pressure

Halved, under ripe
In a separator basket	5 minutes
In a container	8 minutes

Halved ripe, but not too soft
In separator basket	2 minutes
In a container	3–4 minutes

Sliced
In separator basket	1½ minutes
In a container	3 minutes

Pears in Red Wine Peel 4 firm pears, cut lengthways into halves and remove cores and stems. Remove trivet and place pear halves, dome-sides uppermost, on the base of the cooker. Sprinkle with about 40 g/1½ oz caster sugar. Pour over 300 ml/½ pint red wine and 10 ml/2 tsp lemon juice and add 2 cloves and 30 ml/ 2 tbsp redcurrant jelly. Fit the lid and bring the cooker to 10 lb/Medium pressure. Cook for 1½/2 minutes, depending on ripeness. Reduce the pressure quickly.

Lift out pears using a slotted spoon. Remove cloves from cooking liquid, then boil rapidly until slightly syrupy. Pour over the fruit. Serve warm or leave until cold, then cover and chill.

PEAS

For general information about cooking Vegetables, see page 150.

Dried Peas Dried peas belong to the category of foods called Pulses, so for general information about cooking them, see page 114.

Whole Dried Peas There is no need to soak whole dried peas overnight, just put them in a basin 1 hour before cooking, pour on boiling water to well cover and leave to soak. Drain off water and put peas into the cooker, without the trivet in place. For every 450 g/1 lb peas, add 900 ml/1½ pints stock or water, plus a ham bone (if available), a chopped onion and carrot and a bouquet garni. Bring to the boil, remove the scum from the surface and adjust the heat so the liquid is just boiling, but the contents are not rising in the cooker. Fit the lid, maintaining the same heat, bring to 15 lb/High pressure and cook for 5 minutes. Reduce the pressure slowly.

Split Peas These do not need any soaking. Cook in the same way as whole dried peas, using the same proportion of liquid, for 3 minutes. Reduce the pressure slowly. Drain well, unless using for soups. To serve as a vegetable, reheat and beat in some butter or cream, salt and plenty of black pepper.

Pease Pudding Roughly purée the peas (cooked as above) and beat in an egg as well as butter and seasoning. Spoon into a heatproof bowl, cover with a double thickness of greaseproof paper. Rinse out the cooker, then pour in 450 ml/¾ pint water. Put the trivet in place, lower in the bowl, using a 'lifting strap' (see page 77), or the separator basket, fit the lid and cook at 15 lb/High pressure for 20 minutes. Reduce the pressure quickly.

Pease pudding is particularly good with gammon, bacon or sausages.

Fresh Peas Cook in a separator basket at 15 lb/High

pressure with 300 ml/½ pint water for about 2 minutes, depending on size and age.

If blanching prior to freezing (see page 25), cook for barely 1 minute.

Commercially frozen peas really need no more than heating through, so just bring to 15 lb/High pressure, then immediately reduce the pressure quickly. The time required for home-frozen peas will depend on their size, and age when picked, but, as a guide give them about 1½ minutes at 15 lb/High pressure. Reduce the pressure quickly.

PEPPERS

For general information about cooking Vegetables, see page 150.

Peppers, especially red and yellow ones, cook very quickly on the trivet in the pressure cooker; coarsely diced or thickly sliced peppers only require bringing to 15 lb/High pressure; the pressure should then be reduced quickly. Halved peppers need about 1 minute at 15 lb/High pressure. Reduce the pressure quickly. Using the pressure cooker to cook peppers has the additional benefit of being fat-free.

Sliced Peppers Sliced peppers will cook in about 30 seconds. Add them to the cooker when 300 ml/½ pint water has already come to the boil. Cook at 15 lb/High pressure. Reduce the pressure quickly.

Puréed Peppers The pressure cooker comes in very handy when you want to purée red peppers for a sauce or soup in a hurry. Pressure cook sliced peppers at 15 lb/High pressure for 1¼ minutes. Reduce the pressure quickly, then purée the peppers with crème fraiche, soured cream or strained Greek yogurt for a vibrant sauce, or dip, to accompany crudités, simple cooked fish, especially trout and salmon, and shellfish.

Stuffed Peppers The pressure cooker is very useful for quickly cooking stuffed peppers. Pour 300 ml/½ pint water or stock into the cooker and fit the trivet in place. Stand the filled peppers on the trivet (cut a thin slice from the base of peppers to make sure they stand upright). Fit the lid, bring to 15 lb/High pressure and cook for 3–4 minutes. Reduce the pressure quickly.

Stuffed Peppers with Tomato Sauce Using a small, sharp knife, cut around the stalks of 4 red or green peppers to remove stalks and make a small hole. Remove seeds and fine white flesh from inside peppers. Cut a thin slice from the base of each pepper. Fry a chopped onion and a clove of garlic in a little oil until softened. Stir in 2 chopped and skinned tomatoes and cook, stirring occasionally, until most of the liquid has evaporated. Stir in 175 g/6 oz cooked brown rice (see page 121), 100 g/4 oz chopped walnuts, some chopped parsley and seasonings. Divide mixture between peppers. Pour the contents of a 400 g/14 oz can chopped, peeled tomatoes and 150 ml/¼ pint water into the cooker and add a bay leaf.

Place the trivet in the cooker. Stand the peppers upright on the trivet, fit the lid and bring to 15 lb/High pressure. Cook for 3–4 minutes and reduce the pressure quickly.

Carefully transfer peppers to a heatproof dish. Sprinkle a little cheese over tops and place under a hot grill until golden and bubbling. Meanwhile, remove the trivet from the cooker and boil tomatoes mixture hard to make a sauce. Remove bay leaf and check seasoning. Serve with the peppers.

PHEASANT

For general information about cooking Meat, see page 83.

Hang pheasant by their necks in a cool place for 4–7 days before plucking and drawing. For extra flavour, and to tenderize them, the birds can then be marinated in wine, herbs and spices, if liked. Depending on how well you like the flesh cooked, a bird weighing approximately 900 g/2 lb will take about 12–15 minutes to cook, if not pre-browned, and 1.25 kg/2½ lb bird about 15–18 minutes. If pre-browned, take 2–3 minutes off the timings.

Pheasant with Juniper and Lime Remove the trivet from the cooker, add a little oil and, when hot, a chopped onion and 2 crushed garlic cloves, and cook, stirring occasionally, until softened. Put 2–3 crushed juniper berries in the cavity of a bird weighing about 1.25 kg/2½ lb, then add pheasant to the cooker and fry over a high heat, turning occasionally, until lightly and evenly browned. Transfer to absorbent kitchen paper to drain. Pour off excess fat from the cooker, but leave behind the onion and garlic and any sediment. Stir in 4 crushed juniper berries then, after about 30 seconds, stir in 30 ml/2 tbsp gin, 175 ml/6 fl oz each medium bodied, dry white wine and veal or chicken stock, and a bay leaf. Bring to the boil, add the pheasant, fit the lid and bring to 15 lb/High pressure. Cook for about 15 minutes. Reduce the pressure quickly.

Transfer pheasant to a warmed serving plate. Add 15 ml/1 tbsp lime juice to the cooking liquor and boil until reduced. Taste and adjust the seasoning, adding a little more lime juice, if necessary. Gradually swirl in a couple of small knobs of butter, if liked. Serve with the pheasant.

PIES

The pressure cooker can be used for the preliminary cooking of fillings for pies, particularly meat, poultry, pulses or fruit, and, in a few cases, for cooking the covering when this is made from mashed or sliced vegetables, such as potatoes, celeriac, parsnips or Jerusalem artichokes.

Chicken, Ham and Mushroom Pie Quickly brown 4 skinned chicken portions in hot butter and oil in the base of the cooker. Transfer to absorbent kitchen paper. Add 1 chopped onion and a crushed garlic clove and sauté for 3–4 minutes. Stir in 100 g/4 oz thickly sliced, closed cup mushrooms; cook for 1–2 minutes, then add 100 g/4 oz cooked ham, cut into large chunks, a bay leaf, 20–25 ml/4–5 tsp chopped parsley and freshly ground black pepper. Place chicken on top and pour in 150 ml/ ¼ pint each chicken stock and medium bodied, dry white wine, or 300 ml/½ pint stock.

Place the trivet on the chicken, then lay about 575 g/ 1¼ lb thickly sliced celeriac, or potatoes on the trivet. Fit the lid and bring to 15 lb/High pressure. Cook for 6 minutes. Reduce the pressure quickly.

Purée the celeriac or potatoes with 25 g/1 oz diced butter and 60 ml/4 tbsp milk, cream or soured cream. Season to taste. Remove chicken flesh from the bones and chop coarsely. Blend 15 ml/1 tbsp cornflour with a little water, stir into the cooker and bring to the boil, stirring. Simmer for 2 minutes. Remove from heat, discard bay leaf and add chicken. Check seasoning. Pour into a warmed, heatproof serving dish, cover with the celeriac, or potato purée, then sprinkle about 50 g/2 oz grated cheese over the top. Place under a preheated grill until golden and bubbling.

PIGEONS

For general information about cooking Meat, see page 83.

Both farmed and wild pigeon can be cooked in a pressure cooker, but the tenderness of the latter will be improved if marinated overnight in wine, beer, cider, yogurt or citrus juice and herbs. One or more vegetables may also be added, such as chopped onion, carrot, celery and leek, and spices like juniper berries and peppercorns, added for extra flavour; the marinade can be used for the cooking liquid.

Pigeons are usually cooked on the base of the cooker, without the trivet and surrounded by at least 300 ml/½ pint liquid, which could be water, stock, wine or dry cider or the marinade. Herbs, spices and vegetables will add flavour to both the birds and the liquid, which can be used to make a sauce to serve with the pigeons. Cook at 15 lb/High pressure, allowing approximately 8 minutes for farmed pigeons; 10–12 minutes for wild ones, depending on size. Reduce the pressure quickly.

Pigeons in Red Wine Season 4 pigeons lightly inside and out and, if liked, put a couple of crushed juniper berries or a small bay leaf in the cavity of each bird. Heat a little oil in the cooker, without the trivet and quickly brown the birds evenly. Transfer to absorbent kitchen paper. Stir a chopped onion and 2 chopped bacon rashers into the pan and cook, stirring occasionally, until onion has softened. Stir in 4 skinned, chopped tomatoes and cook over a fairly high heat for 2–3 minutes. Stir in 150 ml/¼ pint full bodied, red wine and 150 ml/¼ pint veal or chicken stock.

Return pigeons to cooker, fit the lid and bring to 15 lb/High pressure. Cook for about 10 minutes, depending whether farmed or wild pigeons are used. Reduce the pressure quickly.

Transfer pigeons to a warmed serving plate and boil cooking liquor to concentrate the flavours. Adjust the seasonings and pour over the pigeons.

PLAICE

For general instructions about cooking Fish, see page 59.

Whole Plaice It will only be possible to cook one whole fish at a time in the cooker, and check first that the fish will fit into cooker. Sprinkle freshly ground black or white pepper and lemon juice over fish. Pour 300 ml/½ pint water, or fish or vegetable, stock into the cooker and put the trivet in place. Bring to the boil and lay the plaice on the trivet. Fit the lid, bring to 15 lb/High pressure and cook for time given in chart. Reduce the pressure quickly.

Plaice Fillets Roll plaice fillets up, having first sprinkled them with lemon juice, black pepper and some fresh herbs, such as dill, fennel or basil, or spread with soft cheese flavoured with herbs, or pesto, and place, seam-sides down in the separator basket.

Pour 300 ml/½ pint water into the cooker, bring to the boil and lower in the basket. Fit the lid and bring to 15 lb/High pressure. Cook for about 2 minutes. Reduce the pressure quickly.

Cooking times at 15 lb/High pressure

Whole Plaice, per 450 g/1 lb	4 minutes
Rolled fillets, medium	2 minutes
Stuffed fillets, medium	3 minutes

If fish or vegetable stock is used instead of water for cooking, use it to make a sauce to accompany the fish.

Plaice Fillets with Mushrooms Brush the trivet with oil. Sprinkle both sides of 8 skinned sole fillets with a little lemon juice and black pepper. Lay skin-sides down on the work surface. Mash 175 g/6 oz drained and sieved cottage cheese with the finely grated rind of 1 lemon, a little salt and a dash of Tabasco, then stir in 40 g/1½ oz roughly chopped, peeled prawns. Divide between the fillets, roll them up and secure with cocktail sticks.

Pour 150 ml/¼ pt each water and medium bodied, dry white wine into the pressure cooker and put the trivet in place. Put 225 g/8 oz chopped button mushrooms in the separator basket. Bring the water to the boil, quickly add the plaice rolls and put the separator basket over the fish. Fit the lid, bring to 15 lb/ High pressure and cook for 3 minutes. Reduce the pressure quickly. Transfer the fish to a warmed serving dish, discard the cocktail sticks and keep the fish warm.

Boil the cooking liquor hard in the open cooker until reduced to 45 ml/3 tbsp. Purée the mushrooms coarsely with 5 ml/1 tsp chopped fresh tarragon, or 2.5 ml/½ tsp dried tarragon, the reduced cooking liquor and 45 ml/ 3 tbsp fromage blanc, to give a rough texture. Heat through gently in a small saucepan, stirring, without allowing to boil. Adjust the seasoning and add a little lemon juice, if necessary, to 'lift' the flavour. Serve with the fish. Garnish with sprigs of tarragon and cooked prawns.

PLUMS

For general information about cooking Fruit, see page 61.

For pressure cooking, use cooking plums, or ripe, but firm eating varieties. Halve and stone the fruit, then either place in the separator basket, or in a heatproof container, preferably in a single layer, and sprinkle with a little sugar and add a flavouring, such as crushed cardamom seeds or grated orange rind, then cover the container with a double thickness of greaseproof paper and tie securely. Put trivet in the cooker, pour in 300 ml/ ½ pint water and bring to the boil. Add the fruit in the separator basket, or use a 'lifting strap' (see page 77) to lower in the container. Fit the lid and bring to 10 lb/ Medium pressure, or 15 lb/High pressure if the cooker has only one pressure control. Cook for the time given in chart, depending on the degree of hardness of plums.

Reduce pressure quickly. Sweeten and flavour, to taste, or use as required.

Cooking times at 15 lb/High pressure
In separator basket   about 1 minute
In a container   2 minutes
Cooking times at 10 lb/Medium pressure
In separator basket   1½ minutes
In a container   3–4 minutes

Plum Crunch Cut 575 g/1¼ lb plums into halves and remove stones. Place plums in a shallow heatproof dish, sprinkle over a very little water and sugar, and add the finely grated rind of 1 orange. Cover and cook as above.

Melt 40 g/1½ oz unsalted butter with 45 ml/3 tbsp golden syrup, then stir in 150 g/5 oz porridge oats, 50 g/2 oz soft dark brown sugar, 25 g/1 oz dessicated coconut and 5 ml/1 tsp mixed spice. Spoon over the plums and roughly level surface. Place under moderate grill until the top is crisp. Serve warm or cold with custard, ice cream, cream or strained Greek yogurt.

PORK
For general information about cooking Meat, see page 83. See also Pot Roasting, page 110 and Casseroling, page 38.

Pork is a tender, lean meat, so lean, in fact, that the more expensive, prime cuts, such as fillet (tenderloin), steaks and slices, are liable to dry out easily when cooked.

The most appropriate candidates for pressure cooking are those that are normally braised or casseroled, such as cubed or sliced shoulder (blade), spare ribs and chops. Whilst it is important always to cook pork sufficiently, when cooking it in a pressure cooker, care must be taken not to overcook as it easily becomes tough and dry to eat.

Trim off excess fat and remove sinews. If prebrowning, do it in a little oil over a high heat for a brief time. Make sure the liquid is boiling when pork is added to cooker and time the cooking accurately. Reduce the pressure quickly.

Cooking times at 15 lb/High pressure

Pot roast	
(per 450 g/1 lb meat)	10 minutes
Casseroles (large chunks)	3 minutes
Chops and steaks,	
about 3 cm/1¼ inch thick	4–5 minutes

Pork Goulash Sauté 2 chopped onions and a finely crushed garlic clove in the base of the cooker, in a little butter and oil, until the onion has softened. Stir in 575 g/1¼ lb boned shoulder pork, cut into large chunks and 150 g/5 oz thickly sliced, closed cup mushrooms and cook, stirring, over a high heat for 1–2 minutes. Lower the heat, sprinkle 15 ml/1 tbsp paprika pepper over and stir to coat meat, then sprinkle over 5 ml/1 tsp each caraway seeds and marjoram. Stir in 300 ml/½ pint veal stock, 15 ml/1 tbsp tomato purée, 450 g/1 lb skinned and chopped tomatoes and 2 bay leaves.

Fit the lid, bring to 15 lb/High pressure and cook for 3–4 minutes. Reduce the pressure quickly. Strain off the liquid (keep the meat and vegetables warm) and boil until lightly thickened. Stir the meat and vegetables into the liquid. Transfer to a serving dish and stir through 60 ml/4 tbsp soured cream or cream.

POTATOES

For general information about cooking Vegetables, see page 150.

Old potatoes: peel and cut into quarters, slices or cubes.

New potatoes: wash, if necessary. Leave whole if small, or cut into halves if medium or large.

Cooking times at 15 lb/High pressure

Old, quartered	about 2–4 minutes
Old, sliced or cubed	about 2 minutes
Par-cooked quarters for roasting	2 minutes
New, whole small, or halves	about 4 minutes

POT ROASTING

For general information about cooking Meat, see page 83.

Before starting, check that the piece of meat will fit easily inside the cooker, with the trivet in place. A 1.4 kg/3 lb joint is about the absolute maximum size for even cooking. Longer cooking will also mean that the level of liquid will be higher than is really desirable, and the shrinkage of the joint, which is always greater than when conventionally pot-roasted, will be even more severe.

Trim off excess fat from the meat and calculate the cooking time. Both the flavour and tenderness of the meat will benefit if it is marinated, preferably overnight, in wine, beer, cider, or citrus juice, or, with the exception of gammon and ham joints, plain yogurt, herbs and seasonings.

Lift meat from the marinade, allowing the excess to drain off, and if pre-browning, dry well with absorbent kitchen paper. Remove the trivet from the cooker. If liked, the joint can be quickly browned in a little hot oil, in the cooker before cooking under pressure. Transfer the joint to absorbent kitchen paper and pour off fat from the cooker. Calculate the amount of liquid (water, stock, wine, beer or cider) that will be needed, allowing 300 ml/½ pint for the first 15 minutes cooking time and 150 ml/¼ pint for every subsequent 15 minute period.

Return the trivet to the cooker, place the joint, fat-side uppermost, on it, together with some carrots, onion, leeks and celery, if there is room and herbs or flavourings such as peppercorns and juniper berries, to give additional flavour. Fit the lid, bring to 15 lb/High pressure and cook for the estimated time. Reduce the pressure quickly.

Serve the cooking liquid with the meat, or use it to make a sauce (see page 139) but skim the fat from the surface first. The vegetables that have been cooked with the pot roast will be very soft, so can be puréed with the liquid, or discarded, as wished.

For crisper vegetables to serve with the pot roast, put them into a separator basket; reduce the cooker pressure quickly about 5 minutes before the end of the cooking time, or for as long as the vegetables will take to cook. Open the cooker and add the basket of vegetables. Return cooker to pressure and cook for the required length of time. Reduce the pressure quickly.

PRESERVES

Pressure cooking is ideal for making preserves as not only does it save time, but it is an easy and sure method and produces preserves that taste and look good, as the fruit retains its flavour and colour well.

Only pressure cookers that are fitted with a three-pressure gauge are suitable. Pressure cooking takes the place of the often lengthy, first boiling that is necessary to soften the skin of fruit and break down the cell walls to release pectin (the enzyme that makes preserves set). Very soft fruits such as strawberries and raspberries, only need a brief boiling, so there is little benefit to be gained from using a pressure cooker.

For preserves with a good flavour and clear, bright colour, only use fruit that is ripe and in good condition. Wash carefully if dirty or there is a likelihood it has been sprayed with herbicides or pesticides.

Remove the trivet before adding the fruit and water, making sure the cooker is no more than half-full. Fit the lid, bring to 10 lb/High pressure and cook for the required time. Reduce the pressure slowly .

The base of the cooker can then be used as an ordinary saucepan, and because of the thickness of the base, is ideal. The lid of the cooker must not be fitted. Add warmed sugar to mixture in cooker, generally 450 g/1 lb for every 450 g/1 lb fruit, and heat gently, stirring with a wooden spoon, until the sugar has dissolved. Bring to the boil, skim the scum from the surface and boil rapidly, (skimming the surface occasionally to keep the preserve clear), until setting point is reached, usually between 5–20 minutes, depending on the type of fruit.

There are three ways to test for setting as follows.

1) The most accurate method is to use a sugar or jam thermometer. Warm the thermometer before putting it in in the preserve to make sure that the glass does not break. Stir the preserve, then put in the warmed thermometer, but do not let in touch the bottom of the pan. When the pressure has reached setting point, the temperature will be 105°C/221°F.

2) Flake test: remove the cooker from the heat, dip a wooden spoon into the pan, then spoon up a little of the preserve. Allow it to cool slightly, then allow it to drop back into the pan. Setting point has been reached when drops of jam run together along the edge of the spoon, to form flakes that break off sharply.

3) Saucer test: Chill a saucer in the refrigerator or freezer. Remove the cooker from the heat, then put a little of the preserve on the cold saucer, leave it to cool slightly, then push the surface with a finger. If the surface wrinkles, setting point has been reached.

Pour the preserve into warm, dry, clean jars and cover with discs of waxed paper (waxed-sides down) and dampened cellophane. Secure with elastic bands or string. Label and store in a cool, dark place.

To adapt recipes for pressure cooking, the ratio of fruit to sugar remains the same (usually 450 g/1 lb sugar for every 450 g/1 lb fruit) but reduce the liquid by about half.

See also Jams, page 68, Jellies, page 70 and Marmalade, page 82.

PRE-STEAMING

To ensure pudding mixtures that contain raising agents are light and risen, they are given a pre-steam before being brought to the full cooking temperature, see page 113.

Pre-steaming is done with the lid on the cooker, but without the pressure weights or rotating valve in position, and with the control knob of an automatic cooker set to steam release. Keep the heat low so that the steam will escape gently through the vents. At the end of the pre-steaming period, place the pressure weight or rotating valve in position, or turn the steam release control knob of an automatic cooker to 'closed', and bring the cooker to 5 lb/Low pressure. Cook for the required length of time, then reduce the pressure slowly.

PRUNES

Natural, untreated prunes that normally reqire soaking overnight, need only 10 minutes soaking if cooked in a pressure cooker.

Remove the trivet from the cooker. Use 600 ml/1 pint boiling liquid, such as water, dessert wine, fruit juice or tea, per 450 g/1 lb prunes. Pour over the fruit and leave to soak for 10 minutes. Check that the cooker is no more than half-full, and use a minimum of 300 ml/½ pint of liquid. Fit the lid, bring to 15 lb/High pressure and cook for 5 minutes. Reduce the pressure quickly.

Prunes that have been treated to make soaking unnecessary will be cooked in about 2½ minutes, depending on brand.

Prune Whip Cook 350 g/12 oz prunes as above. Using a slotted spoon, lift prunes from the cooker. Boil cooking liquid until well reduced; reserve. Remove prune stones; leave the fruit to cool, then purée with 150 ml/¼ pint natural yogurt. Add about 30 ml/2 tbsp lemon, lime or orange juice to flavour and 'lift' the purée. Whisk 2 egg whites until stiff but not dry, then lightly fold into purée until just evenly blended. Spoon into serving dishes, cover and chill well. Chill the juice and serve as a sauce with the whip.

PULSES

See also Dried Peas, page 100, Lentils, page 77 and Butter Beans, page 34 etc.

Cooking pulses in a pressure cooker not only cuts down the cooking time, but eliminates the need for the lengthy soaking that beans and peas (with the exception of split peas and lentils) require.

Put the beans or peas in a large bowl, pour over plenty of boiling water so they are well covered, cover and leave to soak for 1 hour. Strain off the water. The liquid used for soaking pulses can cause flatulence, so, if wished, discard it and use 900 ml/1½ pints fresh water, or stock, for every 450 g/1 lb pulses. Otherwise, make up the soaking water to the required volume.

Remove the trivet from the cooker, add water, stock or the reserved liquid and bring to the boil. Add pulses, making sure the cooker is no more than half-full as the water tends to froth and boil up. Do not add any salt at this stage as it will toughen the pulses. Return the water quickly to the boil, skim the surface and adjust the heat so the contents are boiling gently but not rising in the cooker, to prevent blocking of the safety valve. Fit the lid and, maintaining the same heat, bring to 15 lb/High pressure, except for lentils, which should be cooked at 5 lb/High pressure. Adjust the heat so the pressure is just maintained, and cook for the required time. Reduce the pressure slowly.

PURÉES

Vegetable purées have many uses – as well as serving as vegetable accompaniments, they can be made into pâtés, terrines, croquettes, rissoles, 'cakes' and dips; or used for soups, sauces, and for thickening sauces.

Cooking vegetables on the trivet in the pressure cooker produces good, dry purées with a good flavour. Prepare and cut up the vegetables as normal, and cook as stated, see relevant entries, allowing slightly longer cooking time if you usually cook vegetables so they are crisp. Purée in a blender or food processor; pass through a sieve or mouili legume, or mash with a potato masher. Use immediately, or keep in a covered container in a cool place for later.

When finishing the purée for serving as vegetables, heat gently and beat in some butter, milk, cream, fromage blanc, mayonnaise or egg yolks, plus seasonings, and a flavouring, such as orange rind with turnips; fresh tarragon with courgettes; mustard with leeks; nutmeg with cauliflower. Also, try combining purées, such as potato and celeriac, carrot and swede, or broccoli and pea.

Carrot Pudding Coarsely purée 275 g/10 oz cooked carrots, then mix with 300 ml/½ pint milk, 2 beaten eggs, 50 g/2 oz just melted, unsalted butter, 30 ml/2 tbsp finely chopped parsley, or some grated fresh root ginger, and seasonings. Pour into a 1.1 litre/2 pint heatproof basin, cover the top of the basin with a double thickness of greaseproof paper and tie securely in place. Put the trivet in the cooker, pour in 450 ml/ ¾ pint water and bring to the boil, then, using the separator basket or a 'lifting strap' (see page 77), lower the basin onto the trivet. Fit the lid, bring to 15 lb/High pressure and cook for 23 minutes. Reduce the pressure slowly. Leave the pudding to stand for a few minutes before serving.

Parsnip Moulds Purée 400 g/14 oz cooked parsnips with 150 ml/¼ pint double or single cream or milk (or 70 g/2½ fl oz each strained Greek yogurt and fromage frais), 4 eggs, 60 ml/4 tbsp lemon juice, if cream is used, and only 30 ml/2 tbsp for the milk or the fromage frais combination. Add seasonings and grated nutmeg, to taste. Divide between 4 individual, buttered, heatproof dishes. Cover tops of dishes with greaseproof paper and tie in place.

Put the trivet into the cooker, pour in 300 ml/½ pint water and bring to the boil. Using the separator basket, or a 'lifting strap' (see page 77), lower the dishes into the cooker, fit the lid and bring to 15 lb/High pressure. Cook for about 4 minutes. Reduce the pressure quickly. Remove dishes from cooker and leave to stand for a few minutes before unmoulding.

Fruit Purées For the preparation of fruit for sauces, see page 61. Fruit purées can be used to make ice creams and sorbets, and a multitude of desserts, such as fools, whips, soufflés (see page 13), pies, tarts and crumbles. Or serve with milk and egg puddings, pancakes, waffles and ice cream.

Q

QUEEN OF PUDDINGS

Warm 450 ml/¾ pint milk with 25 g/1 oz diced unsalted butter, the finely grated rind of 1 lemon and 25 g/1 oz caster sugar; strain onto 50 g/2 oz fresh breadcrumbs. Leave to stand for about 30 minutes. Beat in 2 lightly beaten egg yolks and pour into a buttered heatproof dish that will fit inside the pressure cooker. Tie a double thickness of greaseproof paper securely on top of the dish.

Pour 450 ml/¾ pint water into the cooker, fit the trivet and bring the water to the boil. Lower the dish into the cooker using the separator basket, or a 'lifting strap' (see page 77), fit the lid and bring to 15 lb/High pressure. Cook for about 23–25 minutes, then reduce the pressure quickly. Whisk 2 egg whites until stiff but not dry, then gradually whisk in 25 g/1 oz caster sugar. Spread some warmed jam or lemon curd over top of pudding, then pile the egg white on top to cover it completely. Place under a moderate grill until golden on top.

R

RABBIT

For general information about cooking Meat, see page 83. See also Casseroling, page 38 and Pot Roasting, page 110.

Lean, tender, farmed rabbit, which is the type most widely available, is more suitable for cooking in the pressure cooker than wild rabbit, and cuts containing bone, are quite successful, providing the time is kept short. Rabbit flesh off the bone will cook very quickly, and easily becomes dry, unless steps are taken to protect it, such as cutting the meat into large, bite-size pieces and coating perhaps in yogurt, not pre-browning; adding to the liquid when it is boiling, and keeping a close eye on the cooking time.

Joints that are browned initially, should be given the briefest cooking in hot oil.

If wild rabbit is to be pressure-cooked, marinate it before cooking in wine, herbs and seasonings to help to tenderize the flesh. Frozen rabbit should be thawed completely before cooking.

Rabbit with Tarragon and Mustard Spread over 4 rabbit joints 22.5 ml/4½ tsp wholegrain mustard and, if time permits, leave for about 1 hour. Remove the trivet from the cooker, pour in 175 ml/6 fl oz each medium bodied, dry white wine and veal stock; add 2–3 sprigs of tarragon and bring to the boil. Add the rabbit, fit the lid and bring to 15 lb/High pressure. Cook for about 5–6 minutes. Reduce the pressure quickly. Transfer the rabbit to a warmed served plate, cover and keep warm. Remove tarragon and boil cooking juices until reduced by about half. Stir in 150 ml/¼ pint soured cream and 30–45 ml/2–3 tbsp more mustard, and simmer until lightly thickened. Taste and adjust the seasoning and level of mustard, if necessary. Return rabbit to cooker and turn joints over in the sauce to coat. Transfer rabbit and sauce to the serving plate.

REDUCING PRESSURE

The pressure inside the cooker must be reduced before the pressure weight, or the lid are removed. There are two methods used for reducing the pressure, and which one to use is governed by the type of food being cooked. The exact procedure to follow for each method depends on the type of cooker, so check the manufacturer's instruction booklet.

Slowly This method is used when cooking liquid foods, such as pulses, rice and pasta, which are liable to spurt through the valve, or vent, on the sudden reduction of pressure; egg custards and milk puddings as they would curdle; puddings containing raising agents also – or they would sink, and when bottling because otherwise the jars would crack.

Carefully move the pressure cooker from the heat and leave at room temperature for about 10 minutes. If using a non-automatic model, gently lift the weight slightly. When steam ceases to escape and there is no hissing sound, the pressure will have dropped. The weight can then be removed completely and the cooker opened.

If using an automatic cooker, wait until the indicator plunger has dropped so no coloured rings or coloured bands are visible, or the metal plunger in the automatic air vent has dropped to its normal position. The lid can then be removed.

Quickly This method is used when precise timing of the cooking is vital, as when cooking vegetables and fish.

For a non-automatic cooker, stand the cooker in cold water, and allow cold water to run over the top, making sure it does not enter the vent, or valve. When there is no longer a hissing sound, the weight is lifted and the cooker opened.

If using an automatic model, turn the pressure release control to the 'steam', or appropriate, position, which will allow the steam to escape rapidly, and so reduce the pressure. When the coloured rings or coloured bands are no longer visible, or the metal plunger in the automatic air vent has dropped to its normal position, the lid can be removed.

Never try to force off the lid before the pressure has been fully reduced.

RHUBARB

For general information about cooking Fruit, see page 61.

Cut rhubarb into 3.5 cm/1½ inch lengths. Put into a heatproof dish, preferably in a single, or double layer, sprinkle with sugar and any flavourings, such as chopped preserves, or finely grated fresh ginger, finely grated orange rind or a sprinkling of ground cinnamon. Cover with a double thickness of greaseproof paper and tie in place.

Pour 300 ml/½ pint water into the cooker and put the trivet in place. Bring to the boil. Using a 'lifting strap' (see page 77), or the separator basket, lower the dish onto the trivet. Bring to 10 lb/Medium pressure, or 15 lb/High pressure if the cooker has only a single control. Reduce the pressure at once and quickly, or cook for about 30 seconds, depending on the thickness of the stems, and how soft you wish the rhubarb to be.

Rhubarb and Ginger Parfait Cut 450 g/1 lb rhubarb into 3.5 cm/1½ inch lengths and put into a heatproof dish with the juice and finely grated rind of ½ orange and 2 chopped, thin slices of preserved ginger, Cover and cook as above. Tip the rhubarb into a non-metallic sieve and leave to drain. Chill the juice. Beat the fruit until pulpy. Beat together 175 g/6 oz medium-fat fromage blanc, 45 ml/3 tbsp caster sugar and 15 ml/1 tbsp orange liqueur, brandy or whisky. Gently fold in the rhubarb. Divide between 4 small stemmed glasses. Chill. Serve with a little of the cold juice spooned over and accompanied by ginger biscuits.

RICE, LONG-GRAIN

Rice cooks most quickly in the base of the cooker, but if you wish to serve it with other food that is being pressure cooked, the rice can be cooked at the same time if placed in a covered, solid container which can be placed on top of the other items.

To cook rice in base of cooker Remove the trivet, bring 900 ml/1½ pints of water, or stock, for each 100 g/4 oz rice, to the boil in the base of the uncovered cooker. Stir in the rice, and salt to taste. Make sure the cooker is no more than half full. Stir well, bring to the boil, adjust the heat so the water is boiling but the contents of the pan are not rising, fit the lid and bring to 15 lb/High pressure, over the same heat. (Rice tends to rise and froth up during cooking, and may block the safety vent.) Adjust the heat so the pressure is just maintained and cook as given in chart. Reduce the pressure slowly. Drain the rice and flavour and season to taste.

Cooking times at 15 lb/High pressure

Long-grain white rice	2 minutes
Long-grain brown rice	3 minutes

To cook rice in a container Use a suitable, wide, deep, ovenproof dish that will fit inside the cooker, or line the separator basket with foil, if only a very small amount of rice is to be cooked. Put the rice into the container and add boiling salted water, or stock, in the proportions of 1 cup of rice to 2 cups of water. Cover the container with foil or a double thickness of greaseproof paper and tie securely in place. Put the trivet in the cooker, if not placing the container on meat or poultry, and pour in 300 ml/½ pint water. Stand the container on the trivet and bring to 15 lb/High pressure and cook as given in chart. Reduce the pressure slowly. Drain the rice well.

Cooking times at 15 lb/High pressure

Long-grain white rice	5 minutes
Long-grain brown rice	8–12 minutes

See also Basmati Rice, page 20.

RICE PUDDING

For general information about using Milk in the pressure cooker, see page 84.

Remove the trivet, bring to the boil in the base of the cooker 600 ml/1 pint milk and a knob of unsalted butter, if liked. Stir in 50 g/2 oz pudding rice, 30 ml/2 tbsp sugar and flavour with a good pinch of cinnamon or mixed spice, or a few drops of vanilla essence and a pinch of grated nutmeg. Return to the boil, then adjust heat so milk simmers gently. Fit the lid and, over the same heat, bring to 15 lb/High pressure. Adjust the heat so the pressure is just maintained and cook for 12 minutes. Reduce the pressure slowly. Stir the pudding and pour into a warmed serving dish. Brown under a hot grill, if liked.

Instead of the spices and vanilla essence, give the pudding a slightly exotic flavour by stirring in a few drops of rose water after cooking; or add a few spoonfuls of double cream for a really luxurious treat.

S

SAFETY

All pressure cookers are fitted with safety features which will come into operation, allowing excess pressure to be released automatically, if the air vent becomes blocked or if the cooker boils dry and overheats.

Check with the instruction booklet supplied with the

cooker to find out what particular features are fitted to the model you have, and always make sure that all steam or pressure outlets are working freely each time before using the cooker.

SAGO

For general information about using Milk, see page 84.

Remove the trivet, bring to the boil in the base of the cooker 600 ml/1 pint milk. Stir in a knob of unsalted butter, 47 g/1¾ oz sago, 50 g/2 oz sugar and a good pinch of cinnamon or mixed spice, or a few drops of vanilla essence and a pinch of grated nutmeg. Return to the boil, stirring, then adjust heat so milk simmers gently. Fit the lid and, maintaining the same heat, bring to 15 lb/High pressure and cook for 2–3 minutes. Reduce the pressure slowly.

Stir the pudding and serve topped with a spoonful of jam or golden syrup, or pour over jam, lemon curd or fruit in a warmed serving dish and brown under a hot grill. If wished, pour the sago pudding into a warmed serving dish, sprinkle with a good layer of soft brown sugar and place under a hot grill until a rich golden brown.

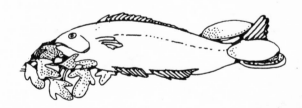

SALMON

For general information about cooking Fish, see page 59.

Salmon is a comparatively firm-textured fish and cooks quite well in the pressure cooker. Cutlets, steaks and fillets are more suitable than whole pieces, such as a middle cut. Cook at 15 lb/High pressure for about 3–4 minutes, depending on size and thickness.

Salmon with Watercress Sauce Sprinkle black pepper and lime or lemon juice over 4 salmon cutlets or steaks.

Put the trivet into the cooker, pour in 175 ml/6 fl oz each medium bodied, dry white wine and fish stock, or 350 ml/12 fl oz fish stock. Add a finely chopped shallot and bring to the boil. Add the salmon, fit the lid and bring to 15 lb/High pressure. Cook for 3–4 minutes. Reduce the pressure quickly.

Transfer the salmon to a warmed serving plate. Boil the cooking liquor hard until reduced to about 175 ml/ 6 fl oz. Meanwhile, remove the coarse stems from a bunch of watercress. Purée watercress with 150 g/5 oz soft cheese and the reduced cooking liquor. Return to the cooker and heat gently, stirring with a wooden spoon, but do not allow to boil. Adjust the seasoning and add a little lemon juice, if necessary, to 'lift' the flavour. Pour around the salmon and garnish with watercress leaves.

SEMOLINA

For general information about using Milk, see page 84.

Remove the trivet, bring to the boil in the base of the cooker 600 ml/1 pint milk and a knob of unsalted butter, if liked. Stir in 47 g/1¾ oz semolina, 30 ml/2 tbsp sugar and a good pinch of cinnamon or mixed spice, or a few drops of vanilla essence and a pinch of grated nutmeg. Return to the boil, stirring, then adjust the heat so the milk simmers gently. Fit the lid and, over the same heat, bring to 15 lb/High pressure. Adjust the heat so the pressure is just maintained, and cook for about 1½ minutes. Reduce the pressure slowly.

Stir the pudding and pour into a warmed serving dish. Or, beat 2 egg yolks into the hot pudding and pour into a warmed heatproof or ovenproof dish. Whisk the egg whites until stiff, but not dry, then gradually whisk in 50 g/2 oz sugar. Spoon onto pudding, covering the surface completely. Place under a moderate grill, or in an oven pre-heated to 190°C/375°F/gas 5, until browned.

SOUPS

Base pressure cooked soups on Stocks, see page 131, for the best flavour, and use fresh ingredients rather than left-overs. As there is very little evaporation of water, add about a third less liquid than when cooking soups in the conventional way and be sparing, initially, with the seasonings, adjusting them before serving. Add enriching and thickening ingredients such as egg yolks and cream, at the end of the cooking.

The cooker should never be more than half-full, but you can still use the cooker to make a larger quantity of soup, by simply using only a proportion of the liquid when cooking the soup, then adding the remainder before serving. Reduce the pressure quickly when making thin soups, but slowly if pulses, grains or pasta have been added, and if milk has been used.

See also Pastas, page 94, Pulses, page 114 and Vegetables, page 150.

Country Vegetable Soup In the base of the cooker, heat a little oil, add 2 sliced onions and 3 chopped smoked bacon rashers and cook, stirring occasionally, until onions are softened but not coloured. Add a thickly sliced red pepper, 2 carrots, 2 sticks of celery and 2 leeks (all cut into large chunks) and cook, stirring, for about 1 minute. Pour in 600 ml/1 pint vegetable, veal or chicken stock, or water, add the contents of 225 g/8 oz can plum tomatoes, 2 bay leaves and 5 ml/1 tsp mixed dried herbs. Fit the lid, bring to 15 lb/High pressure and cook for about 5 minutes. Reduce the pressure quickly. Adjust the seasonings. Garnish with chopped chives or parsley and serve with crusty Granary or wholemeal bread.

SOYA BEANS

For general information about cooking Pulses, see page 114.

Pour sufficient boiling water over the beans to well cover and leave to soak for 1 hour. Drain, reserving the liquid if it is to be used for cooking the beans, and make up the required volume with water or stock.

Remove the trivet from the cooker, add beans and 900 ml/1½ pints water, stock or the reserved soaking liquid for every 225 g/8 oz beans. Do not add salt until after cooking otherwise it will toughen the beans and hamper the absorption of water. Bring to the boil, remove the scum from the surface, adjust the heat so the liquid is boiling, but the contents of the cooker are not rising. Fit the lid and bring to 15 lb/High pressure, over the same heat. Adjust the heat so the pressure is just maintained, and cook for 15 minutes. Reduce the pressure slowly. Drain the beans; flavour and season to taste.

Soya Bean Savoury Soak and cool 200 g/7 oz soya beans as above. Reduce the pressure slowly. Drain, reserving 150 ml/¼ pint cooking liquor. Weigh out 90 g/3½ oz of the beans and purée with the reserved cooking liquor.

Heat a little oil in the cooker, add a chopped onion

and cook until softened. Stir in 5 ml/1 tsp each ground cumin and paprika and cook for about 30 seconds, then add the whole soya beans and cook for 1–2 minutes. Stir in 400 g/14 oz tomatoes, skinned and chopped, 150 g/5 oz sliced mushrooms, the puréed beans, a scant 5 ml/1 tsp dried oregano and salt to taste. Bring to the boil, then simmer for 4–5 minutes. Remove from the heat, and stir through 75 g/3 oz grated mature Cheddar cheese. Serve immediately topped with a spoonful of natural yogurt, sprinkled with paprika.

SPAGHETTI

For general information about cooking Pasta, see page 94.

In the cooker Remove the trivet from the cooker, pour in 2 litres/3½ pints salted water for every 225 g/8 oz dried spaghetti and bring to the boil. Add spaghetti, stir and bring to the boil. Adjust the heat so the water is boiling but the contents of the cooker are not rising, fit the lid and, over the same heat, bring to 15 lb/High pressure. Cook for 1–2 minutes, depending on thickness. Reduce the pressure slowly.

Drain the spaghetti and toss with olive oil, freshly

grated Parmesan cheese, chopped parsley and freshly ground black pepper.

In a container Break spaghetti into shorter lengths. Put into a deep, wide, heatproof container that will fit inside the cooker. Pour on plenty of boiling salted water, add 15 ml/1 tbsp oil to help prevent the spaghetti clumping together, stir, then cover the container with a double thickness of greaseproof paper and tie securely in place. Using a 'lifting strap' (see page 77), or the separator basket, lower the container into the cooker containing 300 ml/½ pint boiling water. Fit the lid and bring to 15 lb/High pressure. Cook for 2–3 minutes. Reduce the pressure slowly. Drain the spaghetti.

Spaghetti, Tomatoes, Olives and Capers Cook 275 g/10 oz dried spaghetti as above. Meanwhile, cook in a small saucepan, for 5 minutes, 45 ml/3 tbsp virgin olive oil, 1 or 2 chopped garlic cloves, 4 skinned and coarsely chopped tomatoes, 10 stoned black olives and 15 ml/1 tbsp rinsed and dried capers (preferably preserved in brine, not vinegar). Drain the spaghetti, reserving a little of the cooking water. Add 12 torn fresh basil leaves to the sauce and season to taste. Toss thoroughly with the spaghetti, adding a little of the reserved cooking liquor if it seems too dry. Serve with grated Parmesan cheese, if liked.

SPICES

Because of the short cooking times, when using a pressure cooker, spices will not soften to become more subtle, and the individual flavours of blends of spices will not mellow and merge. This means that spices used with meat and poultry, will not add much flavour to the dish. However, to overcome this, wherever possible, prepare and cook dishes in advance: meat and poultry can be marinated in the spices before cooking, and, if possible, the dish cooked (or, preferably, slightly undercooked) the day before required, then allowed to

cool and kept, covered, in a cool place overnight. It can then be gently heated through thoroughly when required.
Spiced Chicken Heat 15 ml/1 tbsp each crushed coriander seeds and cumin in a small, heavy pan for 2–3 minutes, then pound with a peeled 2.5 cm/1 inch piece of fresh root ginger. Work in 10 ml/2 tsp each turmeric, chilli powder and garam masala and 20–25 ml/4–5 tsp oil. Spread over 4 chicken portions, cover and leave in a cool place for 3 hours.

Heat a little oil in pressure cooker, add the chicken, a thinly sliced onion and 4 crushed garlic cloves and cook over a fairly high heat to lightly colour the outside of the chicken. Transfer chicken to absorbent kitchen paper.

Pour 300 ml/½ pint chicken stock into cooker, bring to the boil, add the chicken, fit the lid and bring to 15 lb/High pressure. Cook for 6 minutes. Reduce the pressure quickly.

Remove the chicken and keep warm. Boil the liquid in the open cooker to thicken. Adjust the flavourings, if necessary. Lower heat and add the chicken, turning it over in the sauce to coat evenly.

To allow the spicy flavour to mature, reduce the cooking time above to 4–4½ minutes, reduce the pressure and transfer the chicken to a container. Pour the liquid over, leave to cool, then cover and refrigerate overnight. The next day, heat the chicken through thoroughly with the sauce, then transfer the chicken to a warmed dish and finish as above.

SPONGE PUDDINGS

For information about cooking Steamed Puddings, see page 130.

You can use any of your favourite recipes, or other steamed sponge pudding recipes you would like to try. Simply follow the basic procedure for cooking steamed puddings and use the cooking times given in chart.

Cooking times at 5 lb/Low pressure

	Pre-steaming	Cooking
Individual puddings	5 minutes	15 minutes
600 ml/1 pint pudding	15 minutes	25 minutes
900 ml/1½ pint pudding	25 minutes	35 minutes

Cooking Frozen Uncooked Sponge Puddings Provided the pudding is in a suitable container and suitably covered, see page 130, follow the instructions for cooking steamed puddings, adding an additional 150 ml/¼ pint water and allowing an extra 15 minutes pre-steaming, and an extra 10 minutes cooking time for a 900 ml/1½ pint pudding. Reduce the pressure slowly.

Cooked Frozen Sponge Puddings Provided the pudding is in a suitable container, and suitably covered, pour 450 ml/¾ pint cold water into the cooker, place the pudding container on the trivet, fit the lid, bring to 15 lb/High pressure and heat the pudding for 20–30 minutes, according to size.

Canned Steamed Puddings May be cooked in the unopened can. Remove a detachable label and stand can on the trivet, in the cooker. Use 900 ml/1½ pints water as when cooking a normal steamed pudding, but cook at 10 lb/Medium pressure, for a third of the recommended boiling time on the can. Reduce the pressure slowly.

Basic Sponge Pudding Beat together 100 g/4 oz butter or margarine and 100 g/4 oz caster sugar until light and fluffy. Gradually beat in 2 lightly beaten eggs. Sieve together 175 g/6 oz self-raising flour and a pinch of salt, then, using a tablespoon, lightly fold into the egg mixture, adding a little milk to give a soft, dropping consistency, if necessary. Transfer to a buttered 900 ml/1½ pint pudding basin. Cover the top of the basin with a double thickness of greaseproof paper, or a single sheet of greaseproof paper and one of foil, both pleated across the centre to allow for the expansion of the pudding. Tie on covering securely with string.

Place the trivet in the cooker, and add at least 900 ml/ 1½ pints water, plus a few drops of lemon or vinegar. Bring to the boil, lower in the pudding using the separator basket or a 'lifting strap' (see page 77), fit the lid without the weights in place, or with the pressure control knob open, and pre-steam (see page 113) for 25 minutes. Then bring the pudding to 5 lb/Low pressure and cook for 40 minutes. Reduce the pressure slowly. Unmould the pudding onto a warmed plate and serve with custard, cream or ice cream.

Variations

Lemon Add the finely grated rind of 1 lemon to the pudding mixture and spoon some lemon curd onto the base of the basin before adding pudding mixture.

Chocolate Blend 60 ml/4 tbsp cocoa powder to a smooth cream with 15 ml/1 tbsp hot water, then gradually work into the butter and sugar mixture, and if liked, stir in 25 g/1 oz chocolate dots or chips.

Ginger Sieve 5 ml/1 tsp ground ginger with the flour, and fold 25 g/1 oz chopped preserved stem ginger into the mixture. Place 30 ml/2 tbsp golden syrup and 2–3 knobs of unsalted butter, if liked, on the base of basin before adding pudding mixture.

Raisin Add the finely grated rind of 1 orange to the pudding mixture and put some raisins on the base of basin with a little brown sugar and ground cinnamon, plus some knobs of unsalted butter.

STEAMED PUDDINGS

The pressure cooker comes into its own for cooking traditional steamed puddings.

Any type of heatproof basin, mould or other container that is undamaged and will fit inside the cooker can be used. It can be metal, enamel, glass, earthenware or boilable plastic. The recommended cooking times are for puddings cooked in an ovenproof or earthenware basin; if a metal container is used, reduce the cooking time by approximately 5 minutes. Grease the inside of the container well and do not fill it more than two-thirds full to give the pudding mixture room to rise during cooking. The basin should be covered with a double thickness of greaseproof paper, or a single sheet of greaseproof paper and one of foil, both pleated across the centre to allow for the expansion of the pudding. Tie on the covering securely with string to make sure it does not come off during cooking, and so block the safety vent.

Place the trivet in the cooker, to raise the pudding off the base of the cooker, and add at least 900 ml/1½ pints water, plus a few drops of lemon or vinegar to prevent discoloration of the cooker. To lower the container from the cooker, use either the separator basket, or a 'lifting strap' (see page 77). Do not allow the water to boil rapidly for any length of time before the cooking is commenced, or to pre-steam the pudding for too long, otherwise there will be too great a loss of water and the cooker may boil dry before the end of the cooking time.

To ensure pudding mixtures containing raising agents are light and risen, they are given a pre-steam before being brought to the full cooking temperature, see chart.

To adjust normal cooking of steamed puddings, also follow the chart.

Normal steaming time	Pre-steaming	Pressure cooking at 5 lb/Low pressure
30 minutes	5 minutes	10 minutes
1 hour	15 minutes	25 minutes
2–3 hours	20 minutes	50–60 minutes

STOCK

A good stock makes all the difference to many dishes, such as soups, casseroles, pot roasts and sauces, whilst rice, other grains and pulses cooked in a good stock will have so much more flavour. Stocks are very easy to make, but many people are put off making them simply because of the lengthy cooking. However, with a pressure cooker, this drawback is removed.

The best stocks are made from fresh bones, but cooked ones can be used: chop the bones. Use only fresh vegetables, and avoid those with pervasive flavours, such as cabbage. Always remove trivet from cooker. The cooker should not be more than half-full after the water has been added, but if you would like to make a larger quantity (perhaps so that some can be frozen for later use), increase all the ingredients except the water, before cooking, then dilute the stock before it is used. Cook at 15 lb/High pressure and reduce the pressure quickly.

Cooking times at 15 lb/High pressure

Fish stock	8 minutes
Vegetable stock	4 minutes
Chicken stock	35 minutes
Veal stock	40 minutes
Brown veal stock	40 minutes
Game stock	40 minutes

Fish Stock Melt a small knob of butter in the base of the cooker, add a small, halved onion, the chopped white part of 1 leek and 50 g/2 oz chopped button mushrooms. Cook over a moderate heat, stirring the pan occasionally, for 4–5 minutes. Add 900 g/2 lb fish bones, heads and trimmings which have been soaked in cold water and rinsed, and cook, stirring, for a further 2–3 minutes. Stir in 150 ml/¼ pint medium bodied, dry white wine and boil until reduced by half, then add a bouquet garni. Stir in 900 ml/1½ pints water. Bring to the boil, remove the scum from the surface, fit the lid, bring to 15 lb/High pressure and cook for 8 minutes.

Reduce the pressure quickly.

Pass the stock through a sieve lined with muslin or cheesecloth, leave to cool, then remove fat from the surface. Makes about 900 ml/1½ pints.

Vegetable Stock Melt a small knob of unsalted butter in the base of the cooker, add a finely chopped onion and the finely chopped white part of 1 leek; cook over a low heat, stirring occasionally, until the onion has softened. Stir in 1 chopped carrot, 5 ml/1 tsp fennel seeds, 2 chopped small tomatoes, a bouquet garni and 2.5 ml/½ tsp white peppercorns. Add 900 ml/1½ pints cold water, bring to the boil, skim the scum from the surface, fit the lid, bring to 15 lb/High pressure and cook for 4 minutes. Reduce the pressure quickly.

Pass the stock through a sieve lined with muslin or cheesecloth, leave to cool, then remove the fat from the surface. Makes about 900 ml/1½ pints.

Chicken Stock Put 900 g/2 lb chopped chicken carcasses and a chopped veal knuckle bone, if available, into the cooker, add about 1.1 litres/2 pints water and bring to the boil. Remove the scum from the surface, add an onion, stuck with 2 cloves, a thickly sliced carrot, a chopped stick of celery, the thickly sliced white part of 2 leeks, and a bouquet garni. Return to the boil, skim the scum from the surface, fit the lid, bring to 15 lb/High pressure and cook for 35 minutes. Reduce the pressure quickly.

Pass the stock through a sieve lined with muslin or cheesecloth, leave to cool, then remove the fat from the surface. Makes about 1 litre/1¾ pints.

Veal Stock Blanch 900 g/2 lb chopped veal knuckle bones for 1 minute. Drain, rinse in cold water, then place in the base of the cooker. Pour in 1.1 litres/2 pints water and bring to the boil. Remove the scum from the top. Add 1 onion, studded with a clove, 1 chopped carrot, 1 chopped stick of celery, the chopped white part of 1 leek and a bouquet garni. Fit the lid, bring to 15 lb/

High pressure and cook for about 40 minutes. Reduce the pressure quickly.

Pass the stock through a sieve lined with muslin or cheesecloth, leave to cool, then remove the fat from the surface. Makes about 1 litre/1¾ pints.

Brown Veal Stock Place 900 g/2 lb chopped veal knuckle bones and trimmings in a roasting tin, pour a little oil over, then brown in an oven preheated to 220°C/425°F/gas 7, or under a hot grill, turning frequently. Stir in a sliced onion, a sliced carrot, the sliced white part of a leek and a sliced stick of celery. Return to the oven, or grill, for 10 minutes until lightly browned. Stir in 75–100 g/3–4 oz mushroom trimmings.

Tip the contents of the tin into the base of the pressure cooker. Place the tin over a moderate heat and stir in 150 ml/¼ pint medium bodied, dry white wine to dislodge the sediment. Boil until reduced by half. Pour into the cooker. Add 450 g/1 lb chopped tomatoes, a bouquet garni and 1.1 litres/2 pints water. Fit the lid, bring to 15 lb/High pressure and cook for 40 minutes. Reduce the pressure quickly. Pass the stock through a sieve lined with muslin or cheesecloth, leave to cool, then remove the fat from the surface. Makes about 1 litre/1¾ pints.

STORAGE OF PRESSURE COOKER

Check that all parts of the cooker, especially the sealing gasket, and rim of the lid, are clean and dry before being put away. Also check that the control vent, or valve, is not blocked. Store the cooker with the lid upturned in it, and take care during storage to avoid damaging the rim of the base, or the lid as a dent or distortion will prevent an effective seal being made, and therefore the cooker from working efficiently.

SUET PUDDINGS

For general information about cooking Steamed Puddings, see page 130 and also Pastry, page 95. The pressure cooker is ideal for cooking suet puddings and suet pastry puddings, such as jam roly poly, as suet needs a long, moist cooking to be light and delicious. You can use any of your favourite suet pudding, or suet pastry pudding recipes, then simply cook them following the basic procedure for steamed puddings, and use the cooking times given in the chart.

Cooking times for	Pre-steaming	Pressure cooking at 5 lb/Low pressure
900 ml/1½ pint pudding	15 minutes	30 minutes
Roly poly pudding	10 minutes	20 minutes
Suet pastry pudding	15 minutes	20 minutes

Cooking Frozen Suet Puddings Whether sweet or savoury, results are much better if frozen uncooked, then thawed before cooking. They are then cooked in the usual way.

Basic Steamed Suet Pudding Stir together 175 g/6 oz self-raising flour, a pinch of salt, 75 g/3 oz shredded suet and 50 g/2 oz caster or brown sugar. Form a well in the centre, then gradually stir in sufficient milk (about 150 ml/¼ pint) to give a soft, dropping consistency. Spoon into a buttered 900 ml/1½ pint pudding basin.

Variations

Apple Add to the dry ingredients a pinch of grated nutmeg and 225 g/8 oz peeled and finely chopped or grated cooking apples.

Fig and Almond Add to the dry ingredients 100 g/4 oz chopped dried figs, 25–50 g/1–2 oz chopped almonds and the grated rind of 1 lemon.

For a lighter pudding Replace half the flour with 75 g/

3 oz fresh white breadcrumbs.

Roly Poly Pudding Stir together 150 g/5 oz self-raising flour, a pinch of salt and 65 g/2½ oz shredded suet. Stir in sufficient water to make a light, elastic dough. Turn onto a lightly floured surface and knead very lightly until smooth. Roll lightly to an oblong, checking that the width is about 2.5 cm/1 inch less than the diameter of the cooker. Spread the filling over the oblong, leaving the edges clear. Brush the edges with milk or water then roll up, from a short end. Wrap the roll loosely (to allow for expansion), but securely in a single, large, pleated sheet of foil. Seal the ends of the foil very tightly. Put the trivet in the cooker and pour in 900 ml/1½ pints water and a few drops of lemon juice. Bring to the boil. Using 2 foil 'lifting straps' (see page 77), lower the roll into the cooker. Fit the lid without the weights in place, or with the pressure release knob open. Pre-steam, see page 113 for 10 minutes, then cook for 30 minutes at 5 lb/High pressure for 30 minutes. Reduce the pressure slowly.

Variations

Jam Spread the oblong of pastry with approximately 60 ml/4 tbsp jam.

Syrup Add the finely grated rind of 1 small lemon to the dry pastry ingredients; spread the oblong of pastry with 60 ml/4 tbsp golden syrup mixed with 30 ml/2 tbsp breadcrumbs.

Lemon Add the finely grated rind of 1 lemon to the dry pastry ingredients; spread the oblong of pastry with 60–75 m/4–5 tbsp lemon curd.

Mincemeat Add the finely grated rind of 1 orange to the dry pastry ingredients; spread the oblong of pastry with 60–75 ml/4–5 tbsp mincemeat.

Spotted Dick or Dog Use 65 g/2½ oz each self-raising flour and fresh white breadcrumbs. Add 40 g/1½ oz caster sugar, 150 g/5 oz currants, the finely grated rind of 1 lemon and use milk to mix to a dough. Shape into a roll and cook as above.

Suet Pastry Pudding Stir together 150 g/5 oz self-raising flour, a pinch of salt (plus freshly ground black pepper, if making a savoury pudding) and 65 g/2½ oz shredded suet. Stir in sufficient water to make a light, but not sticky dough. Turn onto a lightly flavoured surface and knead very lightly until smooth. Divide off ¼ quantity and reserve. Roll the larger portion out to a circle large enough to line a 900 ml/1½ pint pudding basin. Line the basin with the dough, then roll out the reserved dough to make a circle to cover the top. Spoon in the chosen filling, or see Pork and Orange Pudding, below. Place the dough lid on top and seal the edges together. Cover the top with a circle of greaseproof paper pleated across the centre, then a piece of pleated foil. Tie securely in place.

Place the trivet in the cooker, pour in 900 ml/1½ pints water and a few drops of lemon juice. Bring to the boil, lower in the basin, using a 'lifting strap' (see page 77), or the separator basket. Fit the lid, without the weights in place, or with the pressure release knob open, and pre-steam for 10 minutes, then bring to 5 lb/Low pressure and cook for 30 minutes. Reduce the pressure slowly.

Pork and Orange Pudding Soak 50 g/2 oz dried apricots, then drain, reserving 60 ml/4 tbsp of the soaking liquor; chop the fruit. Gently cook a diced rasher of bacon in a non-stick pan until fat begins to run. Add a finely chopped onion, cover and cook gently, shaking pan from time to time. Add 575 g/1¼ lb lean, diced pork and 50 g/2 oz sliced mushrooms and cook, uncovered, stirring occasionally, for 2–3 minutes. Add the apricots and reserved soaking liquor and the finely grated rind of 1 orange. Remove from heat and add 30 ml/2 tbsp sweet madeira or sherry. Add black pepper and leave to cool.

Add 7.5 ml/1½ tsp finely crushed cardamom seeds to prepared dough. Fill the 900 ml/1½ pint pastry-lined basin with the pork mixture, then cover with the dough lid, pressing the edges well together to seal.

Cover the top with a circle of greaseproof paper pleated across the centre, then a piece of foil or a cloth 'cap' and tie securely in place. Place the trivet in the cooker, pour in 900 ml/1½ pints water and bring to the boil, stand the pudding basin on the trivet. Fit the lid, without the weights in place or with the pressure release knob open. Pre-steam for 10 minutes, then bring to 5 lb/Low pressure and cook for 30 minutes. Reduce the pressure slowly.

The suet pastry dough can also be made into a delicious pudding – see the following recipe idea.

Fruit Pudding Layer about 625 g/1 lb 6 oz fresh fruit (apples, apples and blackberries, plums, rhubarb – prepared as necessary) with 50–75 g/2–3 oz sugar in a pastry-lined basin. Cover with pastry lid. Pre-steam and cook for the times given in Suet Pastry Puddings, see page 134.

SWEDE

For general information about cooking Vegetables, see page 150. Peel the swede and slice or cut into cubes, place in the separator basket and add to the cooker when the liquid is boiling. Fit the lid and bring to 15 lb/High pressure and cook for time given in chart. Reduce the pressure quickly. Toss with unsalted butter and freshly ground black pepper or freshly grated nutmeg.

Cooking times at 15 lb/High pressure

2.5 cm/1 inch cubes	about 5 minutes
1 cm/½ inch slices	3 minutes

SWEETCORN

For general information about cooking Vegetables, see page 150.

Corn on the Cob Remove the green outer husk, and fine silks. Cook in the separator basket, or on the trivet. Pour 300 ml/½ pint liquid into the cooker, bring to the boil, add the corn, fit the lid and cook for time given in chart.

Cooking times at 15 lb/High pressure

Small	about 3 minutes
Medium	about 5 minutes
Large	about 8 minutes

Kernels Canned or frozen sweetcorn kernels require no more than heating through, or the minimum of cooking, so only need to be brought to 15 lb/High pressure. Reduce the pressure quickly.

T

TAPIOCA

For general information about using Milk, see page 84.

Remove the trivet, bring to the boil in the base of the cooker 600 ml/1 pint milk. Stir in a knob of unsalted butter, 45–55 g/1¾–2 oz pearl tapioca, 50 g/2 oz sugar and a good pinch of cinnamon or mixed spice, or a few drops of vanilla essence and a pinch of grated nutmeg. Return to the boil, stirring, then adjust the heat so the milk simmers gently. Fit the lid and, maintaining the same heat, bring to 15 lb/High pressure and cook for 3 minutes. Reduce the pressure slowly. Stir the pudding and pour into a warmed serving dish (put some jam, lemon curd or fruit in the bottom, if liked). Brown under a hot grill, if liked.

Fluffy Tapioca Pudding For a richer, yet lighter pudding, stir 2 egg yolks into the cooked pudding. Whisk the egg whites until stiff but not dry, then fold carefully into the pudding until just evenly blended. If liked, either brown under a preheated grill, or place in an oven preheated to 190°C/375°F/gas 5 for about 20 minutes.

Chocolate Tapioca Pudding Stir chopped plain chocolate, or chocolate polka dots, into the cooked pudding.

THICKENING THE LIQUID

When making soups, casseroles, braises and pot roasts, thicken the liquid after the cooking has been completed. The liquid that has been used for steaming or 'boiling' meats, poultry, fish and vegetables, can also be thickened to make a sauce.

The liquid can be thickened in a number of ways:

★ By boiling it until reduced and the flavours concentrated. The liquid can then be enriched by whisking in cream, butter or soft cheese (see page 115).

★ By puréeing with vegetables. If the liquid has little flavour, reduce it before puréeing. The vegetables can either be ones that have been used in the cooking, or other cooked vegetables. The sauce should then be reheated (see page 115).

★ By puréeing with cooked pulses, then reheating. If the liquid has little flavour, reduce it before puréeing.

★ By puréeing with, or mixing in, breadcrumbs or ground nuts. If the liquid has little flavour, reduce it before puréeing.

★ By puréeing with, or mixing in, chopped block creamed coconut. Reheat the liquid slowly, stirring – do not allow it to boil. See following recipe.

Chicken in Coconut Sauce Mix together 30 ml/2 tbsp each ground coriander and ground cumin, and 10 ml/ 2 tsp ground turmeric. Spread over 4 chicken portions. If possible, cover and leave in a cold place for 2–4 hours. Return to room temperature 30 minutes before cooking.

Remove the trivet from the cooker. Add a little oil, a chopped onion and 100 g/4 oz salted peanuts and cook, stirring occasionally, until browned. Pour in 350 ml/ 12 fl oz chicken stock, 45 ml/3 tbsp lemon juice and 45 ml/3 tbsp chopped parsley. Bring to the boil, add the chicken, fit the lid and bring to 15 lb/High pressure. Cook for 5–6 minutes. Reduce the pressure quickly.

Transfer chicken to a warmed serving plate. Boil the cooking juices until reduced slightly. Stir in 50 g/2 oz chopped creamed coconut and heat gently, stirring, until lightly thickened. Adjust the seasoning and flavourings. Add the chicken, turn over in the sauce, then place on the serving plate. Pour the sauce over and sprinkle with parsley leaves.

★ Blend flour or cornflour (see below) to a paste with a little cold liquid. Move the cooker from the heat and stir in the paste. Return cooker to the heat and bring to the boil, stirring with a wooden spoon. Simmer for about 3 minutes.

Use 15 ml/1 tbsp cornflour or 22.5 ml/4½ tsp flour to 300 ml/½ pint liquid, to lightly thicken it; 22.5 ml/4½ tsp cornflour, or 30 ml/2 tbsp flour to make a sauce with a pouring consistency.

Sweet and Sour Pork Mix together 30 ml/2 tbsp rice wine, 45 ml/3 tbsp soy sauce, 15 ml/1 tbsp oil, 5 ml/1 tsp five spice powder, 10 ml/2 tsp tomato purée, 7.5 ml/ 1½ tsp grated fresh root ginger, 1 finely chopped onion, and a finely crushed garlic clove. Add 450 g/1 lb lean pork, cut into large cubes, and stir it around gently to coat it evenly. Cover and leave in a cool place for 2 hours.

Heat a little oil in the pressure cooker, add ½ a red and ½ a green pepper, chopped and cook, stirring occasionally, for 2 minutes. Using slotted spoon, transfer to absorbent kitchen paper. Remove the pork from the marinade, allowing excess to drain off, and add to the cooker. Cook, stirring, for 2–3 minutes. Stir in the remaining marinade, 225 ml/8 fl oz chicken stock and 7.5 ml/1½ tsp brown sugar. Bring to 15 lb/High pressure and cook for 4 minutes. Reduce the pressure quickly. Remove the pork and keep warm. Add 10 ml/2 tsp cornflour blended with a little water to the cooker and boil, stirring, without the lid on, until slightly thickened. Adjust the levels of flavourings, lower the heat, add the pork and stir to coat in the sauce.

More ideas for thickening:

★ Melt some butter or margarine in a saucepan, stir in an equal quantity of flour and cook for 2 minutes, remove the pan from the heat, then gradually stir in the cooking liquid. Return pan to the heat and bring to the boil, stirring. Simmer for 2–3 minutes. Use 15–25 g/½–1 oz butter and 15 g/½ oz flour to each 300 ml/½ pint liquid.

★ Blend egg yolks with a little cold liquid, stir in a little of the hot cooking liquid, then pour this back into the remainder of the cooking liquid and heat gently, stirring with a wooden spoon, until lightly thickened. Do not allow to boil. Use 2–3 egg yolks to 300 ml/½ pint liquid.

★ To make quite a rich sauce from a plainish liquid, melt some butter or margarine in a saucepan, stir in an equal quantity of flour and cook for 2 minutes, remove the pan from the heat, then gradually stir in the cooking liquid. Return the pan to the heat and bring to the boil, stirring. Remove the pan from the heat and stir some of the liquid onto beaten egg yolks. Stir this into the liquid. Return to a low heat and cook, stirring, until lightly thickened. Do not allow to boil. Use 22.5 ml/4½ tsp flour, 50 g/2 oz butter and 1 egg yolk to 300 ml/½ pint liquid.

★ To make a rich sauce from a plain liquid, use the same method as above, and whisk some additional butter, preferably unsalted, into the sauce. Add another 50 g/2 oz to 300 ml/½ pint liquid.

★ Blend together equal amounts of butter and plain flour to make a paste, then gradually whisk into the hot liquid, over a very low heat. Bring the liquid to the boil, stirring with a wooden spoon, then boil, still stirring, until thickened. Use 15 g/½ oz of butter and flour to 300 ml/½ pint liquid.

Check the seasonings and flavourings of a sauce after it has been thickened.

TIMER, AUTOMATIC

Some modern models of pressure cooker are fitted with a timer that, if set at the beginning of the cooking, will ring when the time is completed, and automatically vent steam from the cooker. This does not mean that the cooker can be left unattended, as the heat beneath the cooker still has to be turned off as soon as the bell rings (to avoid overcooking), and when using an electric hob, the cooker must be drawn away from the heat to release steam.

TONGUE

Tongue is a smooth meat that needs to be cooked by a moist method. Normally, this involves simmering for quite a considerable time – up to 5–6 hours for a large, fresh ox tongue – but by using a pressure cooker, the times is reduced to 15 minutes per 450 g/1 lb.

Ox tongue, which is the largest, also has the best flavour and when served hot makes a deliciously different main course for a lunch or dinner for 6–10 people, depending on the size of the tongue, and when served cold, it makes a very good centre piece for a buffet.

Boiled Ox Tongue If the tongue has been salted, soak it for several hours in cold water, then rinse, before cooking.

Remove the trivet from the cooker, put in a tongue weighing about 1.5 kg/3½ lb and add 6 black pepper-corns, a large bouquet garni, 2 halved carrots, 2 halved sticks of celery and a quartered onion. Pour in 750 ml/ 1¼ pints water, fit the lid and bring to 15 lb/High pressure. Cook for about 50 minutes. Reduce the pressure slowly.

Lift tongue from cooker and peel off skin. Cut away any gristle and bones using a sharp knife. If serving hot, cut into thin slices. To serve cold, curl the tongue around so that it wil fit snugly inside a 15 cm/6 inch cake tin or dish, pour over some of the cooking liquor, cover and place a heavy weight on top. Leave overnight in a cool place. Unmould to serve. Serves 8–10.

TRIVET

All pressure cookers are supplied with a trivet – a perforated shelf with a very short side, or rim. The trivet is usually placed, rim-down in the base of the cooker to raise foods above the level of the liquid so they can be cooked in steam. It is not, therefore, used for soups and casseroles where it is necessary for the flavours of the

various ingredients to mingle together.

The trivet can also be used as a shelf to separate different foods from each other, such as when a meat dish is cooked in the bottom of the cooker, and vegetables are cooked in steam above it, and so retain their individual flavours.

TROUT

For general information about cooking Fish, see page 59.

Trout can be cooked filleted, or whole, with or without their heads and tails on, but check that the number of whole fish you wish to cook will all fit comfortably into the cooker.

Whole Trout Sprinkle freshly ground black pepper and lemon, or lime juice over the outside of the fish, and in the cavity, and place a sprig of fresh herbs in the cavity. Cook either in a flavoured liquid in the base of the cooker, or on the trivet. If cooking on the trivet, the fish can be wrapped in a rasher of bacon or a blanched spinach, cabbage or lettuce leaf, to protect it from overcooking, and to add flavour.

Trout Fillets Should be cooked on the trivet. Sprinkle with freshly ground black pepper and lemon or lime juice. Fold in half lengthways, or roll up from the narrow, tail end.

Whether whole or filleted, trout can also be cooked in foil or greaseproof paper parcels with some chopped vegetables, herbs, spices, a knob of butter or soft cheese, or some wine or vermouth added for flavour. Increase the cooking time by 2 minutes for whole fish and about 1 minute for fillets. Always add the fish to the cooker after bringing the liquid to the boil. Fit the lid, bring quickly to 15 lb/High pressure and cook for time given in chart. Reduce the pressure quickly.

Cooking time at 15 lb/High pressure

Whole trout	about 4–5 minutes, depending on size
Fillets of trout	about 2½–3 minutes

TURKEY

Whole turkeys are too large to cook in a pressure cooker, but many of the increasing number of turkey portions now available, can be pressure cooked either on the trivet, so they are steamed, or on the base of the cooker, surrounded by a liquid, as when casseroling or pot roasting. However, turkey is a tender, lean meat that cooks quickly and easily becomes dry, and those cuts that do not pressure cook very well are the thin, very quick cooking escalopes, and large pieces such as half breast.

Marinating in yogurt will help to keep turkey moist, and the addition of herbs or spices to the yogurt will add flavour to the meat. Cooking times should be the minimum that is needed to just cook the flesh through. It is better to slightly undercook the turkey initially as it can always be given another minute or so, but do not forget to allow the meat to stand for a little while after removing it from the cooker to allow the heat to even out inside it, and remember that cooking will continue if the turkey is to be kept warm whilst a sauce is made.

Frozen turkey must be allowed to thaw completely before pressure cooking.

Cooking times at 15 lb/High pressure

Large cubes	2 minutes
Turkey drumsticks	about 5 minutes
Thighs	about 6½–7 minutes
Turkey roasts	cook conventionally

Turkey with Tomato and Basil Sauce Without the trivet in place, pour 300 ml/½ pint turkey or chicken stock into the cooker, add a chopped shallot and bring to the boil. Add about 575 g/1¼ lb turkey meat, cut into about 3 cm/1¼ inch cubes. Fit the lid, bring to 15 lb/High pressure and cook for 2½ minutes. Reduce the pressure quickly.

Transfer the turkey to a warmed plate and keep warm. Boil the cooking juices until reduced to 150 ml/¼ pint. Beat together 90 g/3½ oz full fat soft cheese, 65 ml/ 2½ fl oz soured cream and 15 ml/1 tbsp tomato purée. Reduce the heat beneath the cooker and stir in the tomato purée mixture. Add about 1.25 ml/¼ tsp dried basil and heat through, but do not boil. Season to taste and adjust the levels of tomato and basil, if necessary. Add the turkey to the sauce and stir to coat.

TURNIPS

For general information about cooking Vegetables, see page 150.

If possible, use small, young turnips as they are tender and have a delicate flavour. Very small ones can be cooked whole, but others should be halved. Cut older, large turnips into cubes or slices.

Put the trivet into the cooker, pour in 300 ml/½ pint water and bring to the boil. Put the turnips into the separator basket and lower into the cooker. Fit the lid and bring to 15 lb/High pressure. Cook for the required time. Reduce the pressure quickly.

Toss with unsalted butter, lemon juice and freshly ground black pepper or nutmeg, or orange juice and lightly toasted hazelnuts.

V

VEAL

For general information about cooking Meat, see page 83. See also Casseroling, page 38 and Pot Roasting, page 110.

Veal is both a lean and a tender meat, and needs careful cooking to prevent it becoming dry. Marinating in yogurt will help keep it succulent.

The cuts that pressure cook most successfully are slices cut across the shank, sometimes referred to as 'osso bucco' and used for the dish of the same name, and chops. Use joints of less than 900 g/2 lb, unless they contain bone, for pot roasting, and roll escalopes rather than cooking them flat. Give extra flavour, and, if the choice is right, succulence, to escalopes by spreading with, for example, wholegrain mustard, pesto sauce mixed into ricotta cheese, or a moist stuffing.

Cooking times at 15 lb/High pressure

Shank slices,
    about 3.5 cm/1½ inch thick   5–6 minutes
Chops,
    about 3 cm/1¼ inch thick   3½ minutes
Escalopes, rolled   about 3½ minutes
Large cubes   3 minutes
Joints   about 9–10 minutes,
                                              per 450 g/1 lb

Osso Bucco In the base of the cooker, cook 1–2 sliced onions and 2 garlic cloves in a little oil over a low-moderate heat, stirring occasionally, until very soft, but not coloured. Stir in 2 chopped carrots and 2 chopped sticks of celery and cook, stirring, for 1–2 minutes. Pour in 150 ml/¼ pint each medium bodied, dry white wine and veal stock, a 225 g/8 oz can chopped peeled

tomatoes, 15 ml/1 tbsp tomato purée, 1 bay leaf, 1.25–
2.5 ml/¼–½ tsp dried rosemary, and freshly ground
black pepper. Bring to the boil, add about 1.25–1.4 kg/
2½–3 lb knuckle of veal, cut into 3.75 cm/1¾ inch
slices. Fit the lid, bring to 15 lb/High pressure and cook
for 5–6 minutes. Reduce the pressure quickly.

Transfer veal to a warmed serving dish. Boil the
cooking liquid until lightly reduced. Remove from the
heat. Blend 15 ml/1 tbsp flour to a paste with a little cold
water, gradually stir in a little of the cooking liquid. Stir
into the cooker, return to the heat and bring to the boil,
stirring. Simmer for 2 minutes. Season to taste. Return
the veal to the cooker and turn it over in the sauce.
Serve in the dish, sprinkled with 45 ml/3 tbsp chopped
parsley mixed with 1 finely chopped garlic clove and the
finely grated rind of a lemon.

VEGETABLES

Vegetables cook very quickly in the pressure cooker so
there is minimal loss of nutrients. The flavour of
pressure cooked vegetables tends to be quite pro-
nounced, although not necessarily 'fresh'.

The most usual and most successful way is to cook
vegetables on the trivet, or in the separator basket, so
they are cooked by the steam from the liquid rather
than in the liquid itself. The steam in a pressure cooker
is at a higher temperature than 'normal' steam, so the
vegetables will cook more quickly than when conventionally steamed.

When cooked in the liquid, vegetables cook more
rapidly and the outside of the vegetable will quickly
soften and become watery, if cooking is prolonged or
timing not accurate. The size of the vegetables, or the
pieces into which they are cut, are important because if
too large the outside will become overcooked before
the inside is ready. All but small vegetables and tender,
long, slim ones, such as French beans and baby carrots,

cook better if they are cut into halves, quarters, or pieces. With short cooking times, and because vegetables can quickly overcook, speed is of the essence. To ensure vegetables cook evenly, make sure they are all the same size, or cut into even-sized pieces, and the same age. See individual entries for more information.

For the best results, add vegetables to the cooker when the water is already boiling, and always bring the cooker rapidly up to pressure, time the cooking accurately, then immediately reduce the pressure quickly.

A selection of vegetables can be cooked at the same time, either by using the separator baskets, or, for small quantities, in separate groups on the trivet. Age, freshness and size affect the cooking time, as they do when using an ordinary saucepan or steamer, but because it is not possible to check how the vegetables are cooking in a pressure cooker, these factors must be taken into consideration before the cooking is started. Different vegetables can be cooked at the same time by cutting those that require the longest cooking into smaller pieces or thinner slices then the others. If vegetables require very different times, such as potatoes and French beans, cook the potatoes first, reduce the pressure quickly, add the French beans and continue cooking, allowing slightly less time than normal for the potatoes.

Cooking times that are specified should be used as a guide, because older, tougher vegetables will take longer than young, tender ones; vegetables cooked on the trivet will cook more quickly than ones placed in a basket, and, of course, personal tastes vary. If cooking vegetables on the trivet, do not fill the cooker more than two-thirds full.

Be sparing with the salt – in fact, better to add it after cooking. All vegetables, except beetroot (see page 22), are cooked at 15 lb/High pressure, and the pressure reduced quickly. Use the cooking liquid for sauces, soups and casseroles.

Serving steamed, pressure-cooked vegetables, especially if cooked in a separator basket, is much quicker, easier and safer than when conventionally boiled as there is no need to strain them; they can be put straight into the serving dishes.

Vegetable Melange Remove the trivet from the cooker. Over a fairly high heat, heat a little oil in the pressure cooker, add 450 g/1 lb each peeled carrots, turnips and parsnips or celeriac, cut into even-sized large chunks, and 8 large, peeled shallots and cook, turning them over, for 1–2 minutes. Add 300 ml/½ pint vegetable stock (see page 131) and 2 bay leaves. Fit the lid, bring to 15 lb/High pressure and cook for 2½ minutes. Reduce the pressure quickly.

Transfer the vegetables to a warmed serving dish and keep warm. Boil the cooking liquid until reduced by half. Blend together 15 ml/1 tbsp wholegrain mustard, 30 ml/2 tbsp flour and 45–60 ml/3–4 tbsp cold milk. Stir in a little of the liquid, then pour into the cooker with 150 ml/¼ pint milk, and bring to the boil, stirring with a wooden spoon. Simmer until thickened, then reduce the heat and gradually whisk in 50 g/2 oz diced unsalted butter. A couple of spoonfuls of bottled mayonnaise, preferably flavoured with lemon or garlic, can also be whisked in. Season to taste with cayenne pepper and salt. Spoon over the vegetables and toss to coat.

Cooking Vegetable Recipes in Dishes This comes in handy when oven space is limited, or non-existent. Use a container that is heatproof. An oven to table dish saves on washing-up. Cover the dish with aluminium foil or a double thickness of greaseproof paper, and tie the covering securely in place with string.

Potato and Leek Layer Put the trivet in the cooker, pour in 300 ml/½ pint water and bring to the boil. Put 225 g/8 oz sliced leeks into the separator basket, lower into the cooker, fit the lid and quickly bring to 15 lb/

High pressure. Cook for 1 minute. Reduce the pressure quickly.

Peel and very thinly slice 575 g/1¼ lb potatoes and crumble 100 g/4 oz feta cheese, or well-flavoured Wensleydale or grated Cheddar. Place a layer of potato slices on the base of a buttered ovenproof dish. Cover with a layer of leeks and scatter some of the cheese over. Sprinkle freshly ground black pepper, chopped thyme and a very little salt over the potatoes and leeks. Continue the layering, finishing with a layer of neatly overlapping potato slices followed by the last of the cheese. Pour over 450 ml/¾ pint milk. Cover the dish with foil or a double thickness of greaseproof paper and tie securely in place.

Stand the dish on the trivet, in the cooker, fit the lid and bring to 15 lb/High pressure. Cook for 25 minutes. Reduce the pressure slowly. Remove the covering and sprinkle about 40 g/1½ oz chopped dry roasted peanuts evenly over the potatoes. Place under a hot grill until lightly toasted.

Frozen Vegetables Frozen vegetables have already been partially cooked, so need only a little more. They should be cooked from frozen, and placed in the cooker when the water is boiling. Place the vegetables in the separator basket, put 300 ml/½ pint water into the cooker and bring to the boil. When the cooker is full of steam, lower in the basket, fit the lid, bring to 15 lb/High pressure and cook for just under the normal pressure cooking time. Reduce the pressure quickly.

When blanching vegetables for freezing, see page 25.

VENISON

For general information about cooking Meat, see page 83. See also Casseroles, page 38 and Pot Roasting, page 110.

Whole joints for pot roasting, or slices or large cubes for casseroling, from both farmed and wild venison can be cooked in the pressure cooker. The flesh from both types will benefit from marinating (in wine, beer or cider, herbs and flavourings) in a cool place for 4–12 hours. This process helps to tenderize wild venison and to keep farmed venison moist.

Trim away any excess fat and sinews, before marinating. Drain off the marinade and pat venison dry if it is to be browned before pressure cooking, then use hot oil and brown over a fairly high heat for a short time. Transfer the venison to absorbent kitchen paper to drain, pour off surplus fat from the cooker.

Add vegetables (to be used for flavouring), spices, herbs and seasonings, and the cooking liquid – wine, stock or cider. Bring to the boil, add the venison, close the lid and bring to 15 lb/High pressure. Cook for the time given in chart. Reduce the pressure quickly. Transfer the venison to a warmed serving dish. Thicken the cooking liquid, if liked, see page 139.

Cooking times at 15 lb/High pressure
Pot roast,
    per 450 g/1 lb   about 12 minutes
Slices,
    3 cm/1¼ inch thick   about 4–5 minutes
Large cubes   about 3½–4 minutes

Note: Cooking times given in chart are for wild venison, so reduce the cooking times slightly for farmed venison.

Venison and Beetroot Casserole Quickly and lightly brown 450 g/1 lb stewing venison cut into large chunks, in a little oil and butter in the base of the cooker, over a high heat. Transfer to absorbent kitchen paper. Stretch 4 rashers of smoked bacon, then roll up each one tightly. Sauté the bacon rolls, 3 more rashers of smoked bacon, cut into strips, and 1 chopped onion until just beginning to brown. Stir in 5 ml/1 tsp lightly crushed allspice berries and 3 cloves. Cook for 1 minute, then stir in 175 g/6 oz grated raw beetroot. Cook, stirring until lightly browned. Stir in 225 ml/8 fl oz full bodied, red wine and 200 ml/7 fl oz game or veal stock. Return the venison to the cooker, fit the lid and bring to 15 lb/High pressure. Cook for about 4 minutes. Reduce the pressure slowly.

Transfer the venison to a warmed serving dish and keep warm. Boil the cooking liquor until reduced to about 200 ml/7 fl oz. Add 30–45 ml/2–3 tbsp port, or some redcurrant jelly, simmer again for 1–2 minutes, then season to taste. Return venison to cooker to coat in the sauce, then transfer the casserole to the serving dish. Scatter grated orange rind over, to serve.

W

WHITING
For general information about cooking Fish, see page 59.

Whiting has a light, delicate flesh, so needs to be treated carefully to avoid overcooking and disintegration. Cook small whole fish on the trivet; fillets rolled up on the trivet, or in foil parcels with herbs or flavourings, such as diced mushrooms, courgettes, lightly toasted almonds or garlic and herb-flavoured soft cheese.

Cooking times at 15 lb/High pressure
Rolled fillets	1 minute
Fillets enclosed in foil	2 minutes
Small, whole fish	3 minutes

WHOLEWHEAT
Wholewheat cooks well in the pressure cooker. Wholewheat has a nutty taste, and even when fully cooked, the grains have a chewy texture. The length of the cooking time can vary with the age of the grains, and the type of

wheat. Wholewheat can be served as an accompaniment to meat dishes, mixed with vegetables, or made into salads.

Remove the trivet from the cooker, pour in 900 ml/ 1½ pints water for every 450 g/1 lb wholewheat to be cooked, add the wheat and make sure the cooker is no more than half-full. Bring to the boil, adjust the heat so the liquid is boiling but the contents of the cooker are not rising, fit the lid and, maintaining the same heat, bring to 15 lb/High pressure. Adjust the heat so the pressure is just maintained, and cook for 10–15 minutes. Reduce the pressure slowly. Strain the wheat and season and flavour to taste.

Warm Wholewheat and Nut Salad Cook 350 g/12 oz wholewheat as above, and reduce the pressure slowly. While the pressure is reducing, gently fry 3 chopped streaky bacon rashers until the fat runs. Increase the heat, stir in 75 g/3 oz chopped walnuts, 40 g/1½ oz dry roasted peanuts and a scant 5 ml/1 tsp paprika pepper. Cook, stirring occasionally, until the bacon is lightly browned and crisp. Stir in 60 ml/4 tbsp olive oil, 15 ml/ 1 tbsp red wine vinegar and seasonings. Bring to the boil, pour over the wheat and toss together with about ½ a bunch of spring onions, chopped. Serve on raw spinach leaves, or watercress leaves mixed with crisp lettuce leaves.

Y

YOGURT
Dishes that contain yogurt can be cooked in a pressure cooker, but because it is heated to such a high

temperature, steps must be taken to prevent it curdling. Blend cornflour (5 ml/1 tsp to every 350 ml/12 fl oz yogurt used) with 20–25 ml/4–5 tsp water, then stir in the yogurt. Pour into the cooker and bring slowly to simmering point, stirring very slowly in one direction using a wooden spoon. Cook gently, stirring the same way, for a few minutes. Proceed with the recipe.

Turkey in Yogurt Sauce Blend 10 ml/2 tsp cornflour with 4–5 tsp water, then stir in 225 ml/8 fl oz strained Greek yogurt. Pour into the cooker and heat very gently, stirring very slowly in one direction, to just on simmering point. Simmer gently, stirring in the same way, for a few minutes. Pour from the cooker, allow to cool, then stir in 30 ml/2 tbsp soy sauce, 2 finely chopped garlic cloves, 22.5 ml/4½ tsp grated fresh root ginger, 75 ml/3 fl oz orange juice, the grated rind of 1 orange and freshly ground black pepper. Add the turkey, turn to coat in the yogurt mixture, then cover and leave in the refrigerator for 4–8 hours, turning the turkey occasionally.

Return to room temperature ½ hour before cooking. Remove the trivet from the cooker. Heat a little oil in the pressure cooker, add the turkey and marinade, fit the lid, bring slowly to 15 lb/High pressure and cook for 2 minutes. Reduce the pressure quickly. Serve with a garnish of chopped spring onions, accompanied by noodles, rice, potatoes or bread to mop up the juices.

INDEX

THE FAMILY MATTERS SERIES